W9-ARU-434

Homeowner's Quick-repair and Emergency Guide

A Popular Science Book

Homeowner's Quick-repair and Emergency Guide

by Max Alth

Drawings by
Lloyd Birmingham

POPULAR SCIENCE

HARPER & ROW

New York, Evanston, San Francisco, London

Copyright © 1977 by Max Alth
Published by Book Division, Times Mirror Magazines, Inc.

Brief quotations may be used in critical articles and reviews. For
any other reproduction of the book, however, including electronic,
mechanical, photocopying, recording or other means, written per-
mission must be obtained from the publisher.

Library of Congress Catalog Card Number: 77-6558
ISBN: 0-06-010142-3

Third Printing, 1979

Manufactured in the United States of America

TO Char

Mish

Syme

Mike

Arabella and

Mendel, without whom my life

would have far, far fewer emergencies.

Contents

Preface

They say that Eskimos spend their long winters telling each other "what if" stories. The stories run something like this. What if you are on an ice floe and suddenly a large polar bear climbs upon it. What would you do? What if you are in your kayak and an angry walrus bites a hole in your boat. What would you do?

The purpose of the storytelling is twofold: to entertain and lead the listeners and possibly the storyteller into a discussion that will prepare them for emergencies. In this way information and experience are passed on, and solutions to what may well be life and death problems are worked out at leisure.

While this book is not intended for Eskimos, its purpose is much the same, and it is supposed to be reviewed at your leisure. In that way you will derive the greatest possible benefit from it because you will be prepared in case of emergencies. Although there is an old saw that runs "It is never too late to learn," it is not intended that the reader turn quickly to F when he finds his home is on fire. The never-too-late-to-learn homily doesn't hold true for emergencies. To cope successfully with sudden problems, you have to expect such problems and to prepare yourself as best you can by laying out plans and rehearsing your response before the troubles arise.

To this end suggestions and directions have been assembled and organized in alphabetical order. The advice given is based on the general premise that the condition or conditions that arise are unusual and sudden and that you may have to act quickly. It is further assumed that you may not have the correct tools or replacement parts on hand, may not have time to secure them and may not even be able to obtain help; that at this juncture, you and your family are entirely on your own. At such moments more or less immediate action may be necessary if you and your companions are to avoid discomfort, loss of property, and even loss of life. At such times you have obviously to think and act fast. Less obvious is the fact that no one thinks and acts best under pressure, although you may believe you do, having seen countless heros and heroines behave this way in films and TV shows.

The individuals who act most decisively in the midst of calamity are those who have thought out what they would do in such cases. They are people who have actually been telling each other "what if" stories, and who have taken the time and made the unpleasant effort to plan for emergencies.

M.A.

AIR CONDITIONER

Drips water into room. This means that the unit is tilted towards the inside of the house instead of outside. Wedge the unit so that it tilts correctly. If the water continues to enter the room, check to see whether the drain holes at the rear of the unit are open. They may be closed by debris. If they are, clean them.

Noisy. A clogged air filter will sometimes increase the volume of sound a unit makes. If removing the filter doesn't help, unplug the unit, remove the cover and inspect the fans. If they are loose on their shafts, tighten the setscrews or lock nuts. Also look for and remove any paper or leaves that may have been sucked in and are touching the fans. Look for dislocated or rusted-through springs beneath the compressor. Replace them temporarily by stuffing soft rubber or some other soft, flexible material between the compressor and the bottom of the cabinet.

Not sufficiently cold. Hold your hand next to the cool air exhaust. If there is a cold stream of air coming out, the chances are the unit is working properly. The trouble is probably that the outdoor temperature is higher than usual and/or that there are many more people in the room than usual. This means that the unit is being required to produce a greater volume of cool air than it was designed to deliver. If this is the case, nothing can be done.

If no cool air is emanating from the machine, check all the controls. Someone may have set them incorrectly. See that the louvers are open. Remove the filter. It may be clogged and so reducing the movement of air through the air conditioner.

Won't start. See that the unit's plug hasn't been accidentally removed from the electrical outlet. Check to make certain there is power at the outlet by plugging a table lamp into the outlet in question. If the conditioner is powered by 220 volts, check the proper fuses. If there is power at the outlet, try turning the air conditioner quickly on and off a few times before leaving the switch in the on position. Sometimes jiggling the switch this way will get the unit to start.

AUTOMOBILE

There is no such thing as a trouble-free automobile, but there are worry-free motorists. They are drivers who accept the fallibility of their vehicles with equanimity, just as they accept the fallibility of man. These drivers are worry-free because they prepare for their vehicle's inevitable breakdown.

They wear or bring clothing along that will permit them to walk home without a problem or to sit out a blizzard without freezing to death. In the car's trunk they store a half gallon or more of water for man and vehicle, a flashlight, a simple set of tools, friction tape, galvanized wire, a can of charcoal-lighting fluid, a can of brake fluid, extra fuses, extra light bulbs, a large spin-type lug wrench, a small can of Liquid Wrench to loosen stubborn lug nuts, a spare tire filled with air, a jack that they have made certain can be used with the car, and a pair of jumper cables. In the winter the well-prepared motorist adds a little antifreeze to his store of water and places a shovel, a cloth sack half filled with sand, and a pair of metal screens for use beneath his wheel alongside everything else he already has in his trunk. He *never* keeps a can of gasoline in the car because that is very dangerous.

Engine won't crank. Make certain the key is fully inserted. Try turning it a few times as far as it will go without breaking it.

Push the automatic gear-shift lever farther into the start position. Try starting the car with the gear lever in other positions.

If there is still no response, turn the headlights on. If the lights are very dim or completely out, you have a dead battery or a poor connection between the battery cables and the battery posts.

Lift the hood. Tighten the cable connectors if you have the tools. If not, try gently tapping the cable connectors down onto the battery. Use a rock if you have nothing else. Forcing the connectors down on the posts tightens the connection.

To use jumper cables, turn the radios and CB equipment off in both cars. Connecting the two batteries together will produce voltage spikes that may damage the transistors in the equipment. Connect the clip on one cable end to one battery terminal. Connect the clip on the other end of the same cable to a terminal on the battery of the second car. Then connect one clip of the second cable to the second terminal of one battery. This leaves you with one battery terminal and a single clip. Holding this clip in your hand, strike it against the remaining terminal with a rapid, glancing blow. If there is a big flash, reverse the two clips attached to the same battery. If there is no spark, or a very tiny spark, you can safely make the last connection.

To tighten battery cable connectors without tools, tap the connectors gently with a stone.

When the temperature is very low and you believe you car cannot be easily started, spray ether into the carburetor inlet tube.

Start the dead engine the normal way. The engine of the other car does not have to be running. When it has started, keep the engine running at a fair clip (don't race it) until you are certain it is warm enough to start again with the weak battery.

Engine cranks slowly. In normal weather, the only solution is either a push or a booster-battery start using jumper cables as described. In cold weather, lack of battery power can be rectified somewhat by bringing the battery indoors and heating it up. Give it plenty of time to heat thoroughly. A battery at 85° F has about a third more energy available than the same battery at zero degrees.

If you have a car in no better than fair condition and expect a lot of cold weather, it is advisable to keep a can of ether on hand. This is sold in most auto supply shops under a variety of names such as Go or Bust, etc. Store the spray can in your deep freeze during summer months. To use, spray a little on the inside of the tube leading to the air filter. Or better yet, remove the air filter cover and spray a little directly into the carburetor. Replace the cover and start the car as usual. If there is any spark at all in the cylinders the ether will explode and turn the engine over with a "whomp." Don't use too much; you can literally burst the engine.

Incidentally, the error most motorists make in trying to start on especially cold days is that they pump the gas pedal too much. Try to start the car as you would normally. Release the key as soon as the engine catches, then work the pedal slowly but steadily to keep the engine alive. Don't race it, but keep it running fast for several minutes before you relax and release the gas pedal.

Engine cranks fast but won't start. Let the engine turn over no more than two or three times. Wait several minutes—longer if you smell gasoline. What may have happened is that you inadvertently flooded the carburetor by pumping the gas pedal when it wasn't necessary. Then try the engine again, this time (if not before) with just a little gas pedal. If the engine won't start after several revolutions, stop. Lift the hood and examine the engine. See if all the wires are in place.

The quick way to check for the presence of gasoline in the carburetor is to remove the air filter cover and have someone depress the gas pedal. If gasoline has reached the carburetor, you should smell it immediately.

Push the ignition wires into the distributor cap to make certain they are all secure. If the wires are wet, pour kerosene or barbecue-fire lighting fluid over all the wires, the ignition coil, and the distributor. The kerosene displaces the water and so dries the wires.

If you have not checked before, see that you have gasoline in the car. If there is gasoline in the tank, remove the cover from the air filter. Push the gas pedal lever down, or have someone push the gas pedal down. You should see and smell gasoline entering the throat of the carburetor. If not, you know the trouble lies in the fuel pump or fuel filter.

If everything checks out fine, as far as you can see, it is wise to wait another 10 minutes or more. Some older cars start fine when cold or hot but start poorly when warm.

If you can't wait, try starting the car again, this time pumping the pedal and hoping for the best. It may start, it may not. But if you do this without checking everything over first you may simply run the battery down without accomplishing anything. If you check everything as suggested first, you will at least know you have tried every possibility within your experience and the all-out attempt is all you have left.

Push starts. All gear-shift cars can be safely started by pushing in either direction. Some cars with automatic clutches cannot be safely started this way. If you have an automatic, check the owner's manual before you let another car push you. In any event, with an automatic, the car must usually reach a minimum of 30 miles per hour before the engine can be started this way.

If you are being pushed in a car with an automatic transmission, put the gear lever in drive, turn the key on (but not the starter), give the engine a little gas and just wait until it starts. Then signal the pusher car to slow down. Run your engine at moderate speed for at least 10 minutes before you assume that you are safely started and can proceed alone.

Push-starting a car with a manually operated gear shift takes a little skill. When you are being pushed by another car, depress the clutch and put the car in second gear. Signal for the push. When you reach a speed of 15 miles per hour or so—your clutch still depressed—signal for the car behind you to stop. Then release the clutch. Feed the engine a little gas, and when it catches quickly depress the clutch again and shift into neutral. Now run the engine at a moderate speed until it has warmed up and can be trusted to idle. At this point you can drive as you normally would.

When you have developed this push-starting skill you can use it to start a light car on a level road by yourself. First, put the gear shift into neutral. Push the car forward as fast as you can and then jump into the driver's seat. Depress the clutch. Shift into second gear. Release the clutch just long enough to turn the engine over and hopefully start it. The instant the engine catches, depress the clutch and move the gear lever to neutral.

Engine overheats. When the engine temperature warning light is in proper working condition and the air temperature is above freezing, the warning light will go on when the engine overheats. In cold weather, the warning light may not go on, and the first indication of overheating or ice in the cooling system may be steam or water squirting out of the radiator overflow hose.

In either event, the safest course of action, as far as your engine is concerned, is to pull off the road and shut the engine off. If the engine continues to run (in the case of a diesel) put it in gear or move the automatic gear-control lever to reverse. Let the car rest until the radiator cap is cool enough to touch. Even then, use caution when removing the cap as a fountain of hot water may still jump at you. Fill the radiator up with water before moving on.

If you cannot pull immediately off the road, you can continue driving at a slight risk to your engine until you hear a frying sound, or smell oil burning or steam stops coming out of the engine. Go past this point and you will surely damage your engine beyond repair.

There are any number of reasons why an engine overheats. In the winter a frozen radiator is the main cause. At other times, a broken or loose fan belt is the most probable reason for overheating. On hot days you can overheat an engine by running the tires too soft (in which case they drag), overloading the car with passengers and luggage, and/or towing a trailer the car was not designed to pull. Long periods of idling in traffic can also cause overheating in some cars. In such cases shut the engine off when you believe you will have to idle for more than a minute.

If you cannot eliminate the causes of overheating, you can still continue on your journey if you use a little care. Fill the radiator with water. Leave the radiator cap off. Drive off at a moderate speed of 30 to 40 miles an hour. Note the exact time. Watch the signal light. When it goes on, pull off and stop again. Note the time difference. Let the engine cool down. Fill the radiator again. Assuming that the engine boils in 10 minutes, run for 5 minutes, pull over and let the engine cool down. By repeating this sequence of running and stopping you will be able to continue on to your destination without damaging the engine.

Engine lacks power. If the engine is "rough," the chances are that the cause is a defective spark plug or a loose or defective wire. Most gas stations carry the popular plugs, so that is not much of a problem.

To find a defective high-tension wire you have either to replace all the wires or to look at the engine running in the dark. You will see the high voltage jump through the breaks in the defective insulation. If it's neither the plugs nor the wires and the engine put-puts along, missing on a cylinder or two, it is best to stop or at least cut your journey short. If the cause is a stuck exhaust valve, you will burn out the valve and its seat in short order if you continue.

On the other hand, if the engine operates smoothly but lacks power, check the tires. If they are soft, you are losing power there. Next check your air filter. A really clogged air filter can slow you down. If the engine is weak only when going up hills, check your gasoline filter. A clogged filter or a partially defective fuel pump will produce this effect.

Assuming you can find nothing wrong, and the engine, while appearing weak, runs smoothly without overheating, you can continue on your trip with little danger of engine damage, although you may be burning extra fuel. Note that all engines run best on cold, damp days at sea level and worst on hot, dry days at high altitude. Also, since it is difficult to judge engine power by the seat of one's pants, it is possible you may be a little mistaken about loss of engine power.

Brakes fail. With time the master cylinder on a hydraulic brake system wears and its associated valves begin to leak a little. When this happens you will find the brake pedal sinking beneath your foot. To regain braking power you need only release the pedal and push down again. As wear continues you will find that you have to do this more often as the pedal sinks more quickly. However, you will always be able to regain braking power because you have not lost any of the fluid in the system.

When the system develops a small leak, the brakes feel and react the same way. However, you will find that no matter how vigorously you pump the pedal you

A clogged air filter will rob your engine of power and greatly reduce its gas milage. On almost all engines the cover and the filter can be removed.

can never raise it to its previous height. That is because you are losing brake fluid. Depending on the size of the opening in the system, this leaking process can take anything from days to minutes.

Should you think or find that you are losing fluid, pull off the road. Generally you can smell the alcohol in the escaped brake fluid. Inspect the car. If it is only a loose pipe, you can tighten it easily enough. If it is a break in a line, the line has to be replaced. Taping the holes doesn't do much.

If the leak is small, fill the brake reservoir with more fluid. Continue driving, but go very slowly and do not use your brakes unless absolutely necessary. Replace the fluid before the pedal has worked its way down to the floor.

If the leak is large—and a brake hose can be ripped right off when a wheel drops into a deep pot-hole—your brake pedal will go right down to the floor when you depress it. If you need instant braking, pump the brake just as fast and as hard as you can; you may get a little action out of it. If your car has an automatic transmission, put the gear lever in low. Use the hand or parking brake immediately.

Apply as much pressure to the parking brake as you can. If doing so reduces your speed and brings you to a halt, fine. If the parking brake can't stop you, warn your passengers and brace yourself, then move the automatic gear lever into reverse and park. This maneuver may damage the transmission and possibly the car's engine beyond repair, but it is your last hope of slowing the vehicle down and possibly stopping it. Bear in mind the motion will be abrupt, so prepare yourself and your passengers.

If this doesn't stop you, pick a soft target like a bush or a wood fence or scrape the sides of your car against parked cars or the side of a hill. Do this immediately. Do not imagine that you can scoot down a long hill, around corners and across busy intersections, accelerating all the time, without disaster.

If your car has a manually operated transmission, you can't just shift down. If the car is moving too rapidly for the gear you are trying to engage, you will not be able to engage it. To shift down, step on the clutch, race the engine (this is no time to try to match gear speeds) and slip the stick into the next lowest position (from gear 5 to gear 4, let us say). Let the clutch out slowly, with your foot off the gas. Let the engine slow the car as much as it will. Continue shifting down in this way to slow the vehicle up until you are out of gears. Use the reverse only when you are just crawling. And don't fear revving the guts out of the engine to shift down; you have no alternative.

Lights fail. If the lights don't respond to the switch when you first step into the car and the engine won't turn over, you have either a loose battery connection or a dead battery. See the section, "Engine won't crank."

If all the other electrical devices work on the car and the lights don't, you have probably blown a fuse. Replace it. If you don't have a replacement, wrap metal foil around the fuse and reinsert it in the fuse block.

If one light of a pair doesn't work, try tightening and loosening the screws near the lamp and tapping the side of the metal near the lamp. The fault may be the lamp itself and it may be the ground connection. Shaking and tugging sometimes restore the connection, temporarily at least.

If you don't have the correct replacement bulb, try whatever bulb you have, assuming it is also 12 volts. You may not get the light to work the way you want it to, but you may get some light.

If you have no rear light at all, tape a flashlight to the car, with its beam on a portion of the vehicle.

One way to separate a damaged fender from the wheel is to lift the fender with the jack.

Body and fender damage. Usually you can let body and fender damage go until it is convenient for you to make the repair. However, if a fender or another portion of the car's body is deformed to the point where it drags on the wheels or interferes with steering, you must, of course, eliminate the interference before moving on.

One method you might try consists of placing the car's jack beneath the bent part. When you raise the jack you apply the car's weight to the bent fender or damaged hood and so straighten it somewhat. Another possible approach is to use a strong timber, if you have one, to pry the folded metal back to more or less where it belongs.

If a door latch is broken, the door can be tied closed with rope. Hanging fenders can sometimes be lifted clear of the wheels with wire. If necessary, punch a hole through the fender with a nail and a rock, and thread the wire through the hole. You may not look beautiful when you are finished, but you will be mobile again.

Locked out. If you lock yourself out of your car you can try getting back in by lifting the door button with a piece of wire. A wire clothes hanger works fine. Just slip it between the window and the doorframe.

If your car's windows are too tightly fitted into their frames to slip a wire inside and you have keys to the trunk, try getting into the driver's seat from that part of the car. It is easy on some makes of vehicles. If you find you have locked yourself out of your car when you have parked downtown in a large city, try the local police. They jimmy into parked cars all the time, preparatory to towing them off. But first make certain you have proof of ownership with you.

Other emergencies. If you get a flat tire while in a tunnel, on a bridge, or even on a busy highway, do not attempt to change the tire there. Run the car all the way out of the tunnel, off the bridge, and down the highway until you can find a parking place sufficiently clear of traffic even though you may ruin your tire and wheel doing so. A great many people have been killed changing a flat tire on the side of a busy road.

If you have a flat and your jack cannot reach down below the bumper, run your car up on the spare tire. This will enable the jack to be fitted into place. If you have no jack, look for a long, strong tree limb or timber. With it, you can lever the car off the ground. Hold the car up with a concrete block, rocks, or even a metal milk crate.

If you find that you cannot remove the lug nuts holding the wheel in place so that you can change the tire, apply a little Liquid Wrench to the threads of the bolt and rap the side of the nut with your wrench when you do this. The vibration helps the solvent penetrate into the threads. If you have no solvent, remove the oil dip stick from the engine and drip a little oil down into the threads on the bolt. If that doesn't loosen the nut sufficiently to enable you to remove it, and there is a second person present, have him or her work one side of the wrench while you work the other.

If two of you still cannot loosen the nut, have your helper hold the portion of the lug wrench projecting outwards from the nut, while you jump on the side of the wrench, or kick down against it. If you do not have a helper, use a jack to hold the wrench in place while you jump or stomp on it. As a last resort, heat the lug nut with a cigarette lighter to make it expand a little and so loosen it.

If you are driving along and your car starts to act up, do not continue hoping that the trouble, whatever it may be, will disappear. Too many motorists have become stuck that way right in the middle of the road. Pull off the road as soon as the engine starts to miss or lose power. You can always drive back on if the trouble disappears.

If you are female and alone and your car breaks down, don't leave the car and thumb a ride. Don't lift the hood, the universal call for help, supposedly. You do not want to draw possibly unpleasant attention to yourself. Instead, remain in the auto and watch for a policeman. Blow your horn and signal him as he approaches. There is usually a 15- or 30-minute patrol of every highway in the country. If some stranger does stop to offer help, keep your window closed until you can be reasonably certain he or she is there to actually help.

If you don't have a jack, you can raise your car with a plank and some concrete blocks.

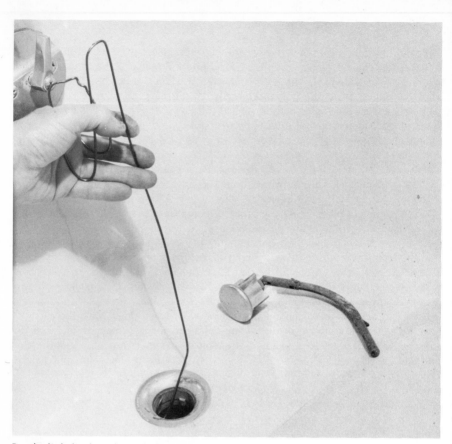

Bend a little hook on the end of a piece of wire and use it to clear a clogged drain when you do not have a suitable snake or drain chemicals.

BATH TUB

Stopper doesn't seal. The water drains slowly out of the tub despite the stopper being in the closed position. Operate the control to lift the stopper to its open position. Pull the stopper out and check to see that no sediment has collected on the lip or the seat which would interfere with sealing and permit the water to leak out. If the seat and lip are clean and smooth, remove the stopper arm and lever and shorten the lever by adjusting the nut and bolt. Replace.

Tub won't drain. If there is no movement of water at all out of the tub, remove the stopper and try poking a wire down the drain. If you bend a little hook on the end of the wire (a piece of a wire coat hanger will do fine), and if you have some luck, you may remove the obstruction. If this doesn't work there is nothing practical to be done until you secure the proper tools and disassemble the tub's trap. You should be able to reach the trap through a trap door behind the tub or from the basement below.

If the water is moving slowly, let it all leave the tub. If you have no drain-clearing chemicals, pour boiling water down the drain. Repeat this several times, each time waiting until all the water is gone.

BEDS

Fallen rail. The ends of the rails (sides) of a wooden bed are usually fastened to the head- and footboards with S-shaped hooks made of flat metal. The hooks are usually riveted to the rail ends. When the rivet comes out, the hook comes out and the rail's end falls to the floor. The proper repair consists of cementing the rivet back in place with epoxy cement. But if you would rather not fool with cement in the middle of the night, use a nut and bolt in place of the rivet.

Fallen mattress. This may be caused by either of the two cleats fastened to the insides of the rails coming loose, or one or more slats (crosspieces of wood) breaking. To refasten the cleats, remove the mattress and spring and replace the loosened wood screws with larger screws.

If a slat has broken, tape a piece of wood across the break. There is very little load on the slats and this will be sufficient.

BEES AND WASPS

All stinging insects are dangerous. The larger insects, such as bees and wasps, are more dangerous mainly because they inject a greater quantity of venom into their victims. The degree of pain and injury suffered varies with the individual in more ways than one.

Some of us are allergic to insect bites and one full discharge from a bee's needle can put us six feet under. Some of us develop a tolerance so that each successive sting hurts less providing there is a goodly period of time between stings. And some of us develop an inner chemical defense that becomes so strong in response to repeated stings that a single sting can be fatal. In other words, we become increasingly sensitive to insect bites as time goes by.

The best emergency response to a bee or wasp sting is still to remove the stinger (it looks like a tiny thorn) and then cover the area with a blob of soft mud. Then cover yourself with a coat or sweater, sit down and rest.

A daub of mud is the best poultice for bee and wasp bites.

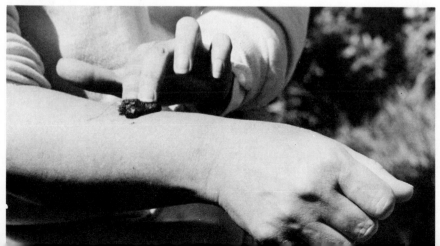

If you feel weak, nauseous, cold (this indicates you are running a temperature) or the bite has swollen to more than a large pimple, don't take chances, go to a hospital. If you have been bitten more than two or three times, go to a hospital. Don't wait for a severe reaction to warn you of danger.

Wasps, hornets, and yellowjackets (they are all variations of the same kind of insect) enter a home most often in the early spring, before you have put up the screens, when a sudden heat wave wakes them from their winter's sleep. Individual bees hardly ever make the mistake of entering a home.

Individual insects. Train your family to respond immediately to the presence of a wasp in the room, to note where the insect has alighted and then to leave the room and *close the door behind them.* Positively the worst thing anyone can do is to run screaming away. This doesn't disturb or anger the insect, it just paralyzes everyone. The danger of a stray wasp in the home is not that it will attack. Fortunately these insects do not attack unless their nest is threatened. The danger is that someone will sit on the insect or put on a piece of clothing containing it. Sitting on it isn't too bad; you may crush it or get no more than a single jab. But when the insect is caught within your clothing and frightened it may sting you half a dozen times before it gives up or loses its stinger in your flesh.

Therefore, you must know where the insect is at all times. If it is flying around in a large room, detail a kid to watch it while you rush for a can of insect spray and a tennis racquet. If the wasp is locked within a room, approach very carefully. Open the door slowly so that you can be certain it does not dart past you unseen. Close the door behind you. If you cannot see or hear the insect, rap the floor with your racquet. Sometimes that will make it move and you can locate it by sound if not by sight. If rapping doesn't move him, try pushing the curtains and shades with your racquet. In cool weather the wasp or yellowjacket will generally head for the window or a portion of a wall that has been warmed by the sun.

When you have sighted the insect, let him alight, sneak up and give him a good shot of the spray. Then use the racquet to hold him in place while the poison takes effect. If you have no patience and cannot wait until the wasp or yellowjacket lands, give him a backhand shot with the racquet, taking care to note where the blow drives him. You don't want an angry insect, dying for revenge, under the covers when you go to bed at night.

Ground nests. Yellowjackets often construct their nests in holes in the earth near a stone wall or an old log. To destroy the nest wait until they have gone to sleep in the evening or go out at early dawn when they are stiff with cold. Then pour a couple of gallons of motor oil (discarded engine oil will do fine) into the hole and over the surrounding area. Then, with a shovel, turn the soil over and over until the oil is thoroughly mixed with the earth and the nest. Do not try this during the daylight when the creatures are active. They will attack en masse.

Mud daubers. These are wasps that build homes of mud against the side of a foundation wall or the corner of a window. In cold weather you can simply scrape the mud nests off and crush them underfoot. In warm weather soak the mud with insect spray. The preparation made for ants and roaches works fine.

Hanging nests. These are nests ranging up to the size of a basketball made by wasps from a sort of rough, gray paper. You will find these nests in unscreened attics, under the eave of a house and hanging from a tree.

When the nest is very small you can sneak up on it and soak it with the insect

Mud wasp hives should be soaked with insect spray in the summer. Wait until winter before destroying the hive.

spray already mentioned without alarming the inhabitants. When the nest is large, this is much too dangerous. Wait until you have reached the depths of winter. Then you can knock the nest down and burn it without fear.

To destroy a large nest in the summer, attack at night, fully protected by heavy clothing, leather gloves, and a face veil. Then soak the nest with any suitable oil-based poisonous solution. Give the poison time to do its work. Then remove the nest and toss it into a large bonfire.

Swarming bees. Call the police. They usually know a local beekeeper who will be glad to hive them for you. Don't approach the swarm yourself unless you are fully protected. If the bees enter a room in your home, give up the room until help arrives. If you cannot find an apiarist to help you and the bees are outdoors and out of the way, let them alone. They will not bother anyone and may move on by themselves. If they are in the way, for example if they have gathered near the front door, build a smoky fire close by. The smoke may cause them to move on.

If the bees are indoors and you cannot get help, explode a bug-bomb or two in the room and close the door. Do not reenter the room until you are certain the bees have fled or have been destroyed.

BLIZZARDS

As officially described, a blizzard is a combination of cold air, heavy snow (4 inches in 12 hours minimum), strong winds, extremely low visibility or no visibility at all. Blizzard warnings are generally broadcast when winds of 35 mph and temperatures of 20° F or less are expected. Severe blizzard warnings mean that winds are expected to reach 45 mph or more and that the temperature will dip below 10° F.

Upon receiving such a warning it is time to check your store of provisions, emergency fuel and gear. If you have outbuildings, such as hen coops, that you must visit, connect a rope hand line between the building and your door. It is only too easy to lose your way in a blizzard, even in your own backyard. If there is someone in your family that may have to visit a doctor or go to the hospital, take them immediately. Once the blizzard hits, the roads may be closed for days. Certainly, no traffic will be able to move during the storm.

If you are at home, the best thing to do during a blizzard is nothing. Sit tight and wait it out. Use your fuel and food sparingly. Close off the rooms you do not need. Move everyone into one room if you believe you may run short of fuel. Turn down the radiators in the unused rooms, and just wait.

If you're in an auto, unless you can clearly see your destination, do not leave the car. Remove your tie. Loosen your shoes and belt. Remove tight undergarments. Tight clothes restrict the circulation of blood and reduce body temperature.

Open one window a fraction of an inch. You must have air. Do not run the engine continuously; you may run out of fuel. But do run it for a few minutes periodically to keep the car's interior temperature above freezing. Don't try to keep it hot; you will waste fuel. Open one door every once in a while so that snow will not pile up alongside and make it impossible for you to leave when the blizzard is over.

If you hear the sound of a rescue party, switch your headlights on and off and blow your horn.

BURNS

Minor burns. Burns such as you might get touching a hot stove or having a drop of hot oil fall on your hand can be prevented from blistering or even hurting very much by immediately placing your burned finger against the ice in the freezer portion of your refrigerator. If that is not possible, hold the injured member under cold running water and keep it there long after the skin is numb.

The human body is about 98 percent water. When the body is heated to blister or burn temperature, not only is the immediate area damaged, but the heat is retained and continues to cause damage and pain. Cooling the body immediately often saves the overheated area from damage and numbs it so that pain is reduced. You will find that merely holding a cube of ice to a burn after you have given the area a cold treatment holds the pain down.

Major burns. The following is the present-day, accepted, and practiced emergency medical treatment for burns. You do not need skill or experience; you just

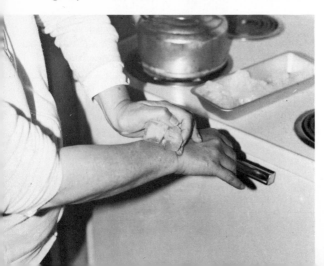

Best aid for all burns is to apply ice or cold water. When the burn area is small, it is sufficient to hold a cube of ice against it.

need speed. So in the case of serious burns, call for help but do not wait for help to arrive. Instead, take the following steps.

Place the victim or just the burned part of the victim's body under a cold shower. If you can remove his or her clothing without removing any skin, do so. If there is any possibility of removing or injuring skin, let the clothing remain but keep the cold water running.

Meanwhile, fill a tub with cold water and ice cubes. Gently immerse the victim totally or partially in the ice water and keep him or her there. If only an arm or leg is damaged, keep the rest of the body warm.

Bear in mind that your major purpose is to cool the injury and numb the body so that the heat can cause no further body damage and pain. Continue with the cold treatment until medical help arrives.

Do not apply oil, butter, chicken fat, honey, or any old-time remedies or even modern unguents to the burned area; just keep it cold. When the pain is gone and nature has begun its healing process you can apply vitamin E oil to the burn to speed healing and reduce the scar tissue.

CAN OPENER, AUTOMATIC

Won't start. Check the wall outlet for power. Examine the plug to make certain all the wires are securely connected. If there is power and the plug appears to be satisfactory, remove the can and press the handle down. If the motor turns, look for something clogging the cutting wheels and remove the obstruction if it is present. If the motor does not turn, remove the plug from the wall and open the unit. Look for disconnected wires and reconnect them.

Can turns very slowly. You may be pressing the control handle down too hard. The cutting wheels may be clogged; if so, clean them. Or the cutter may need to be sharpened. Use a small file to do this. You may also be trying to cut an odd-sized can, or one with an unusually thick lip, in which case the opener can't possibly work properly.

Can turns, but isn't opened. You may have failed to press the control handle down hard enough. Try again. If that is not the cause, look for an accumulation of grime or a chip of metal near the cutter that prevents it from penetrating the can to a sufficient depth to cut the metal. Also look for bent parts. Use a pair of pliers to straighten them if necessary.

CHAIRS

Legs separating from each other. If you have time, clean the ends of the cross braces. Apply glue and reinsert the brace ends into the legs. Then make two clamps by wrapping rope around each pair of diagonally facing legs and twisting the ropes with two short sticks. If you have no time, let the glue go until later and just clamp the legs together. In the case of a stool, you can use wire as a permanent brace and forget the glue.

Legs coming out of the chair's seat. If you have time, remove the legs, clean their ends and apply glue. Reinsert the legs and then drive a wood screw into the joint between the leg and the side of the hole in the bottom of the seat. If you are in a hurry, just use the screw. It will hold the leg in place.

Backrest loose. Whether or not you can use either of the following methods will depend on the construction of the chair and whether or not your emergency repair will prove unsightly.

Turn the chair over. Drill holes through the bottom of the seat up into each backrest side member. Drive a wood screw into each hole. This will not only expand the ends of the side members but will help hold them in place.

If this is not possible, drill holes sideways through the chair seat and into the backrest side members. Drive wood screws through each hole.

CLOTHES WASHER

Won't start. See that all the controls are in the proper positions, required. See that the door or lid closes properly. (Some washers have a safety switch that prevents operation when the door is only partially closed.) If the machine has just satisfactorily finished a large wash and won't start, the cause could be an open thermal safety switch. Wait until the machine is cold and try again. If the machine still will not start, run the timing switch slowly through its positions. If there is no sound, the fuse or circuit breaker in the line has probably opened. Replace or reset as necessary. If there is any kind of sound whatsoever, the machine is receiving power.

Little or no water. The hoses may be kinked and if so should be straightened. The valve at the washing machine connection may be partially closed. If this is the case, open it. The water-inlet screen may be clogged. You will usually find this screen where the flexible hose is connected to the machine. Shut the valve and prepare for a minor flood. Then disconnect the hose at the machine and clean the screen. Another cause of lack of water in the washing machine can be a disconnected, stuck, or defective solenoid water valve. Remove the machine's line plug. Tip the machine over and look for disconnected wires at the solenoid. (You will find it right next to the water connection.) If that is the fault, reconnect the wire(s). If the wires are properly connected, try rapping the side of the valve a few times. That may loosen it.

Too much water. A partially stuck solenoid valve may be the cause. The best emergency solution is to control the flow of water into the machine by operating the hand valves.

Will not spin or stops in the middle of spin cycle. This can be caused by an unbalanced load, in which case shut the machine off and rearrange the clothes.

It can also happen if a cover safety switch is shaken into an open position. The result, with an even slightly unbalanced load, may be a start/stop cycle that blows a fuse or opens the circuit breaker. Try holding the cover down experimentally with your hand for a few moments. If that is the trouble, the switch may be worn to where it has become oversensitive. Use a weight on the cover until you have a chance to replace the switch.

Grinding noise. The noise may be caused by an open drain plug on the transmission which has permitted the oil to drain out. The transmission is running dry and chewing itself up. Stop the machine immediately. Do not resume operation until the cause is found and cured.

Pounding noise. Very loud, regular beats like a slow-march drummer on the big bass are probably caused by too much clothing in the machine or a very unbalanced load. Stop the washer immediately and correct the fault. If you don't, the machine may be badly damaged.

Excessive vibration. This can be caused by a badly overloaded machine and/or an unbalanced load. Reduce the load and/or adjust the clothing evenly around the sides of the tub.

Washer doesn't empty. This can be due to a defective drain pump, in which case there is nothing to be done until you can get a replacement. It can also be caused by a clogged or kinked drainpipe. In some instances the stoppage is due to clothing that has slipped beneath the rotor. Some rotors can simply be lifted up and off. Others have a large nut on top that has to be backed off first.

COOKING IN EMERGENCIES

If your home is served by both gas and electrical lines, you can prepare for the absence of gas by purchasing a single-element electric stove. A multi-element electric stove is even better, but you will be surprised at how much you can do with the single-burner electric stove.

Supplies. Your preparation for the possibility that both services will be out at the same time will depend on what your home presently contains. If you have a fireplace, all you need store is fuel and a means of lighting it. The fuel can be wood, charcoal, or wood and hard coal. If you have no fireplace you can use a hibachi, in which case you will also need half a dozen common bricks in addition to charcoal and lighting fluid. As an alternative, you can store a propane-powered camping stove in your emergency closet.

To make certain you will have the means with which to light your cooking fire, store a quantity of old-fashioned, strike-anywhere wood matches in a watertight container. Better yet, soak the matches in wax before you store them. Not only will the wax keep the matches perfectly dry, it will also add to the flame the match produces. In addition it is wise to store a few wax candles; the plumber's candles are best since they are thicker. The candles will conserve your matches. When you use a lighted candle rather than a match to start a fire, not only do you have much more time—a fat candle will burn for hours—but the flame is larger and hotter, giving you that much more chance of igniting material that is damp and difficult to light.

To prepare for a shortage of food, stock your larder with concentrated, non-perishable foods such as beans, flour, rice, powdered milk, noodles, and dry cereals such as oatmeal and cracked wheat. Canned foods should include meat and fish, preferably in solid form such as spam or tuna rather than as a prepared stew, which normally contains little substance. Delicacies such as canned peaches and canned or bottled jams and jellies are better left out. The sugar content of all these items increases your appetite rather than reducing it (contrary to general opinion). Since you are not going to have an unlimited supply of food there is little sense in storing non-nutritious and hunger-inducing foods.

Neither the dry foods nor the canned foods should be stored and forgotten. The dry foods should be removed, consumed, and replaced at least every 6 months. The canned food should be replaced at least every year.

To prepare for a shortage of water, figure a minimum of ½ gallon of water per person per day in cool climates and 1 gallon per person per day in warm to hot climates. This is drinking and cooking water only. Store the water in the 5-gallon plastic cans made for gasoline. Do not depend on the water remaining fresh for more than a few months. Change it. In addition, purchase water-purifying pills or tablets from a camping supply shop and store them nearby. Use them to purify the water you have stored and whatever water you find available elsewhere.

Cooking over an open fire. Whether you cook indoors in a fireplace or outdoors on the ground do not build a regular fire and attempt to prepare your food by hanging or holding pots above the flame. To do so is to waste a tremendous amount of fuel. The much better way is to set up two small logs about 6 inches apart or a couple of bricks in two parallel lines. The fire is built directly on the hearth or the ground between the two barriers. The pots and pans are then placed on top of the logs or bricks. Outdoors you can dig a trench about 2 feet long, 6 inches deep and as wide. The fire is built inside the trench and the pots are set on top. An alternative method consists of building a small fire directly on the hearth or the ground, letting the fire die down a bit and then setting the pots directly on the fire. This is the most efficient and rapid way of cooking over an open fire.

Build your cooking fire between two small logs or two rows of bricks to conserve fuel and speed cooking (left). An even more efficient way of cooking consists of setting the pot directly on the fire (right).

If you have no fireplace and are unable to go outdoors, you can build your fire in the basement if it has a dirt or concrete floor. Just be certain to open a window for air.

Cooking on a portable stove. If you have a hibachi you can place it in your fireplace, open the damper and cook away. To conserve fuel, don't fill more of the firebox than necessary to cook one burger or to heat one pot at a time. To conserve starting fluid, break a few of the charcoal briquets into small pieces before trying to light them. If you don't have starting fluid, build a small wood fire and then add small pieces of charcoal as the fire comes up.

If you have a hibachi but no fireplace, you can still use it, either on a concrete floor in the garage or cellar, or sitting on a small platform made of bricks. Without the bricks underneath the hibachi will scorch a wood floor and eventually set it on fire. Again, be certain to open a window nearby.

Camp stoves do not require insulation underneath when placed on a wood floor. But they too need plenty of air and should not be placed near curtains or similar flammable materials.

Other stoves. You can make a stove of sorts, often used by kids in my younger days, from any kind of can or pail with a bail handle. Small holes are punched in the bottom of the can and around the sides near the bottom. The can is then filled with a little paper and pieces of wood. A length of rope is tied to the handle. The paper is ignited and with the help of the rope, the can is swung rapidly in a circle. The motion of the can forces air through the fire and the wood is quickly ignited. Charcoal can even be lit in this way. When the fire is going strong the can is set on the ground and whatever you wish to heat is set on top.

An oil-burning stove can also be made from a large tin can. The can is half filled with dry sand. Holes are then punched in its sides above the level of the sand. Then oil or kerosene is poured slowly onto the sand. The oil seeps into the sand. If you have a little gasoline, it may be added, but do not use gasoline alone. Next, a small twist of paper is poked into the oil-soaked sand and lighted. This ignites the oil in the sand, which rises slowly to the surface of the sand as it is consumed.

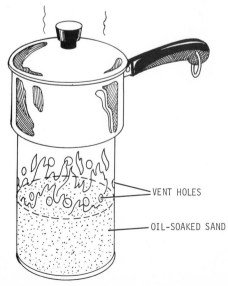

An emergency stove made from a large can.

VENT HOLES

OIL-SOAKED SAND

To remove a few drops of gasoline from the tank of your car,
lower a rope into it.

Fuel. You can use wood in the hibachi if you have no charcoal, and you can use charcoal in an open fire if you start it with either lighter fluid or a small wood fire. You can also burn hard or soft coal and coke if you break them into small pieces and add them to a hot fire. Even green wood will burn if you cut the pieces thin enough.

You can use motor oil, cooking oil, lighter fluid, kerosene, turpentine, and even alcohol in the tin-can stove described.

Lighting the fire. If you have no matches and your pocket lighter is out of fuel, try placing a drop of gasoline or even a little flammable cleaning fluid on its wick. You can remove a little gasoline from your car's tank by lowering a rope into the tank. When you remove the rope, some gasoline will adhere to its end.

When you do try the lighter, be certain to have a piece of paper on hand which you can ignite with the lighter because the lighter's flame is not going to burn for very long. Also, be certain to remove the gasoline-soaked rope a good distance from your fire-making experiment.

If your electric stove is working and you need fire for some purpose you can ignite a strip of paper by holding its end to a turned-on heating element.

If the above methods are not available and your car is handy, try the cigarette lighter.

If this lighter isn't working and your car's battery is not dead you can try the following. You need about 2 feet of thin, bare wire—it can be copper or iron—and a piece of rag soaked in a little lighter fluid or kerosene or if there is nothing else, a little gasoline. The center of the wire is wrapped two or three times around the rag. One end of the wire is connected to one post on the car's storage battery terminal. Then the other end is held in a pair of pliers or with your gloved hand and touched to the second battery terminal. Electricity flowing through the wire will quickly turn it red-hot and ignite the rag.

If the sun is out you can use solar energy to start your fire. You can do this with a suitable lens. The lens from a pair of reading glasses, telescope, binoculars, or camera can be used. Hold the lens between the sun and the tinder you wish to ignite. Vary the distance from the lens to the tinder until you find the lens position that concentrates the sun's rays into a point on the tinder. Hold the lens steady and you will soon have a flame.

Optimal use of available food. While the very suggestion of rationing will immediately make everyone present hungry, the human body will secure more en-

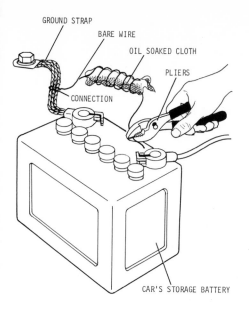

GROUND STRAP
BARE WIRE
OIL SOAKED CLOTH
PLIERS
CONNECTION
CAR'S STORAGE BATTERY

How to convert the electricity in your car's battery to a flame.

ergy (if not gustatory satisfaction) if the available foodstuff is eaten over an extended period of time. Our bodies are highly adaptive. Our digestive process becomes increasingly efficient as the quantity of food we consume decreases. The first step in an emergency involving food is therefore to estimate how long the food must last and then to divide it into time periods. Obviously, if water too is going to be in short supply, it must also be rationed. The second step consists in determining the perishability of your foodstuffs. That which can go bad should, of course, be eaten first.

In hot weather you probably will secure the greatest nourishment from any food by eating it raw. In cold weather you may secure a little more nourishment and energy by eating the food hot. By boiling or stewing everything that can be

Using solar energy to set a thin piece of paper afire. A candle will keep the flame alive.

prepared this way you will feel more satisfied with what food you do consume and you will be able to utilize food that might otherwise not be eaten. Some people are so frozen in their habits that they will go hungry rather than eat something they have never eaten before or do not like. This is not of much importance in a young person, but in the elderly abstinence from food is often accompanied by a refusal to drink that can lead to serious physical deterioration far earlier than the 30 days most people can go without food.

Anything and everything can be made into soup, including such items as bones, gristle, flour, and cereal grains. Just cut the ingredients into pieces, throw them into the pot and let them boil awhile. Salt, pepper, and hunger will make it all taste good.

Do not discard any food unless it is rotten; even then, the rotten portions can be cut off and the rest used. Do not peel potatoes; cut them up and boil them in their skins. Do not discard pea shells; cook and eat them along with the peas. Cut mold on bread away and eat the rest. If the bread is rock-hard, dump it into your soup or stew. If you have the necessary ingredients, bake bread. If you have only flour, mix it with water and eat it that way, or make a dough and either flatten it and bake it right away, or let it stand awhile and give the natural yeast organisms a chance to loosen it a bit before you bake it. If you have any kind of edible oil, mix that with the flour and bake the resultant dough. This will enable you to consume oil that you could not digest easily by itself.

Do not fry, toast, or roast any food when it is in short supply. These methods waste a large percentage of the food.

Don't take culinary chances. Don't eat anything wild that is white unless someone present has spent a lifetime picking, eating, and surviving the food he gathered in the woods. There is absolutely no food value in mushrooms, but there is a good chance that you may unknowingly pick a poisonous one, so why risk it? Generally, if the berry or fruit has a color and tastes good it is edible.

Don't eat from partially opened cans, jars, or other containers in which the food is discolored, soft, mushy, gassy, or doesn't taste right. It is probably poisonous and the chances that the toxins produced by botulinal bacteria can be removed by boiling are very slim.

CYCLONES, HURRICANES, TORNADOES

Cyclones, hurricanes, and tornadoes differ only in degree. They are all unpleasant manifestations of a specific type of storm. As the word "cyclone" denotes, these are all storms characterized by winds rotating about a center called the eye of the storm. Storms involving relatively low wind speeds may be hundreds of miles across with a moderate barometric pressure differential between the edge and the eye of the storm, which may be 5 to 25 miles across. In all cases the wind rotates counterclockwise in the northern hemisphere. The storm as a whole may move at speeds of 5 to 15 miles per hour.

As the speed of the rotating wind increases, the diameter of the storm decreases. When wind speeds in excess of 500 miles per hour are reached, the storm may be no more than a few hundred yards across, and its eye reduced to a few dozen yards in width. When this occurs the barometric pressure within the eye may be twice that of the rest of the storm. As the speed of the circular wind increases, the speed at which the entire storm moves also increases, reaching a top speed of about 40 miles per hour. Fortunately, such violent storms—called "twisters" in Kansas, where they are all too common—usually ease up before they have traveled an hour. During this brief period they literally chew up everything in their path, cutting a clean sweep across the land the way a giant bulldozer might, sometimes destroying just half of a building and leaving the rest untouched. When the eye of the storm passes over a house, the structure often explodes because of the sudden pressure differential.

Preparation. It would appear on reading this or actually seeing a twister—which looks like a black funnel of air reaching from heaven to earth—that nothing in this world can survive in its path. But this is not so. A twister can't reach into a strongly roofed cellar, though it can toss railroad cars about like toys. To be safe in twister country you must prepare a storm cellar for yourself and family. Essentially it is a deep room with a concrete or equally strong roof and a strong, tight-fitting door. Since it may be occupied for days, it must be properly ventilated, lighted, and provisioned. Most important, you need a battery-operated radio so you can keep abreast of the storm's movements.

Buildings are usually protected by strong storm shutters. In place of shutters, sheets of thick plywood may be nailed over the windows and doors.

Tornado watch and warning. Our government spends millions of dollars every year keeping track of hurricanes and tornadoes. When one develops an announcement of a watch is made. This means a tornado is forecast for your area. When you hear this over your radio or TV, keep tuned. The story that is unfolding may be your own. When a tornado *warning* is broadcast, a tornado is heading in your direction. Tornadoes generally follow a straight path, but they can curve to the side at any time. So never ignore an area warning because it may appear as though the tornado is going to miss your home. Take shelter immediately a tornado warning is issued.

Taking shelter. If you are at home and there is time, put up the storm shutters or nail sheets of plywood in place. Open the windows behind them so air can move freely in and out of the house. If you do not have shutters, leave the windows open on the side of the house away from the approaching storm. Take your family into your storm cellar or cyclone cellar as it is called in some areas. If you have no storm cellar, go into your house cellar and make yourself comfortable in its center.

If you are outdoors and there is no building in which you can take cover, lie flat in the nearest ditch or ravine. It will offer you some protection. The danger lies not only in the wind, but in the objects that fly through the air like bullets on the wings of the wind. If you are driving and can see the twister approaching, drive away from it at a right angle. As stated, twister speed is never much more than 40 miles an hour. You can dodge it if you don't panic. If you can't move the car, for one reason or another, or if you are in a parked trailer, don't remain in either of them if you can run to the shelter of a substantial building nearby. The twister can easily destroy an automobile or a trailer. If there is no place better to go, remain in the vehicle, which at least will protect you to some extent from flying objects.

DISHWASHER

Doesn't wash. Start the machine. Stop it in mid-cycle by unlatching and opening the door. If there aren't a few inches of water in the bottom of the machine, see that the water hose is not kinked and that the water shutoff valve in the supply pipe, assuming it is an under-the-counter washer, has not been mistakenly closed by someone. If the valve is open and the water supply pipe is not folded, inspect the float. This is the inverted plastic cup near the front left side of the machine. See that there is nothing beneath it to prevent it from dropping down and closing the switch that operates the solenoid admitting water to the washer.

If you find water in the bottom of the unit and the machine doesn't wash, re-start the washer and stop it again. Open its door and look to see whether or not there is water dripping down from the dishes. If there is not, remove the dishes and then wash your hands free of any dishwasher soap that may have gotten on them, since it will burn them. Disconnect the revolving water arm. With a hollow-shaft nut driver loosen the nuts holding the central plastic screen and water diverter in place. This removed, you will be able to see the top end of the rotary pump on most machines. Try spinning it. If it isn't free, look for a piece of metal or plastic lodged between it and the support. Remove the obstruction if there is one and you are back in business. If this pump doesn't turn, water is not thrown up over the dishes and no cleaning takes place. If the pump is free, the trouble can be a defective timing switch, defective motor, or disconnected wires. You can check for loose wires by turning the machine over.

Doesn't wash clean. Dishwashers are go/no go devices. If there is sufficient water in the machine and the pump is working, the cause of poor washing is not the machine itself. The trouble most likely is one or more of the following: The incoming water is cold; too many dishes have been placed in the machine; the dishes are improperly stacked; the dishes have been kept waiting too long, and the food on them has dried into a glue.

Noisy. The usual cause of excessive noise is improperly stacked dishes banging against one another or a small, lightweight dish being driven around the inside of the washer by the water. Stop the machine, reposition the dishes and remove the flying saucer or pin it down.

Leaks. Water coming out of the dishwasher itself may be the result of a spoon or some similar object being caught between the door and the frame, thus preventing complete door sealing. It may also be caused by something holding the float down, in which case the flow of water into the washer is not shut off until the timer moves on to the wash position. This results in so much water collecting inside the washer that the water leaks past the door seal or pours out when you open the door.

See that the door is free to close tightly. See that the float is free to move up and down as it should. Try the machine again. (Open the washer's door to check when the machine reaches its dry cycle; you don't have to wait through it.) If water leaks out of the machine or if there is water inside when there should be none, the machine is probably not draining properly.

Won't drain. First make certain the trouble really lies in the drain system and not in an inlet valve that won't close. To do this, shut off the machine's supply

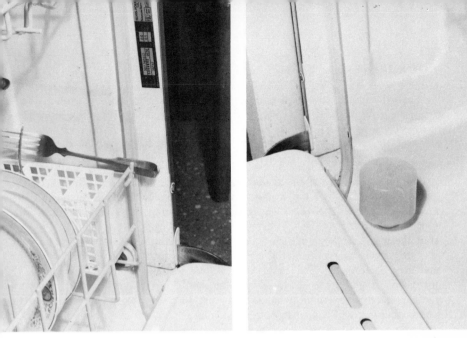

The two most common causes of water coming out of a dishwasher are (left) a fork or similar object lodged between the door and the frame preventing proper sealing, and (right) the water-valve control float stuck in a down position. Here, it is shown free, but a carelessly positioned dish can easily hold it down.

of water by closing the valve in the supply line. Run the machine through its paces. If the water in the machine remains inside, the trouble is in the drain system.

The most common problem is a clogged drainpipe. Open the joint between the washer's rubber hose and the house drain. This is where the debris most often gathers. Clean this area with a snake or a stiff length of wire. Then check the house drain by running a snake down it. If you don't have a snake, use a garden hose.

After you have made certain the drainpipes are not clogged, connect the pipes together again, and then, with the water supply valve to the washer still closed, run the machine through its wash cycle. If upon opening the door to the washer you find all the water has been pumped out, your problem has been solved. On the other hand, if there is still water inside the machine, the drain pump is not working.

Remove the spray arm and plastic apron beneath it to expose the inlet to the drain pump. If this area is clogged as shown, the machine will not drain properly and water will accumulate.

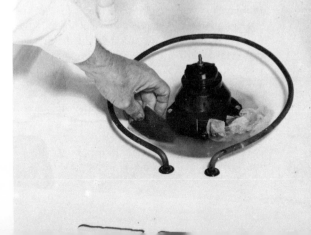

On the older machines, small, individual motors pump the water out of the washer. On the newer machines, one motor is used for washing and pumping. To wash the motor turns in one direction. To pump it turns in the other direction. Since two different coils are used on the one motor for the two directions of rotation, it is possible for the motor to turn in one direction and not the other. None of this will help you repair the motor but it may save you time trying to cure a trouble that can only be remedied by replacing the motor.

Won't start. See that there is nothing between the door and the frame. Check that the door closes all the way and that the locking handle is swung all the way into the closed position. The washer will not start unless this handle closes a switch into the dishwasher cabinet.

If the washer still doesn't start and the timing control is clearly past its start position, check for power at the wall outlet. If there is power here, slowly turn the timer control through all the cycles. Listen to the machine as you do so. If any power is getting to the machine you should hear something. In that way you can roughly determine what is and what isn't working, and if you want to look farther you will have a starting point from which to begin troubleshooting.

DOORS, EXTERIOR

Loose hinges. If the doorframe is not too badly cracked and the door-hinge screw holes in the frame are not too greatly enlarged, force epoxy cement into the crack and the holes. When the cement has partially set, poke a match stick through the center of the old holes. This will enable you to start the screws in the holes when you refasten the door hinge.

When the doorframe is badly cracked, remove the door trim along the hinge side of the frame in order to get behind the frame. Place a board about 1 foot long and 4 inches wide behind the screw holes in the frame. Then drill through the frame. Countersink the holes and, using flat-head wood screws, fasten the board to the frame. Now you can replace the hinge and by using longer screws that enter the back-up board you have fastened, you can tighten the hinge in place.

When the frame is badly battered, as it may well be if a strong wind has ripped the hinges from the frame, fill the space between the frame and stud with wood. Use one or more pieces of wood of various thicknesses to make a snug fit. Drill through the frame and through the boards you have placed there. Next, drive long screws through the frame, through the boards and into the stud. This will hold the cracked pieces of the frame together. Treat the cracks in the doorframe and the enlarged screw holes with epoxy as suggested.

Won't close. See that the weather stripping around the doorframe hasn't been bent out of shape. If that is the trouble, straighten it or remove it so the door can be closed.

Assuming that the weather stripping, if there is any, is not preventing the door from closing, the trouble is either the frame or the door. Frames change from a rectangle to a diamond when one end of the house sags. You can usually recognize this condition by looking through the frame at the almost closed door, or by checking the frame's corners with a steel square. When a doorframe is distorted, the only practical recourse is to cut the edges of the door back to make it fit into the frame.

When the frame is satisfactory the trouble is with the door, in which case it usually takes one of two forms or a combination of both. These are swelling and warping. Both conditions are caused by moisture entering the door as a result of lack of ventilation within the house and lots of open-pot cooking. Generally, swelling and warping are accompanied by peeling paint. If the door is only swollen and you can get by without closing it fully, remove the paint from the inside of the door, ventilate the house and cover the pots. In time the door will shrink back to its original size. If you must close the door, you will have to plane down one edge to make it fit, but be warned that a door can swell as much as ¼ inch in width. This means your door will be that much shy of its frame when it dries out.

If the door is also warped, you have to force it back into shape while it is drying. You can do this with the help of heavy galvanized wire, as shown in the illustration.

Won't latch. This may be caused by the latch bolt sticking in the lock mechanism. If jiggling the doorknob loosens the bolt, spray a little powdered graphite into the lock mechanism. Do not use oil.

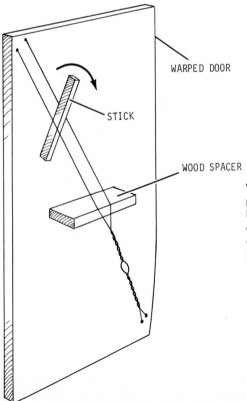

WARPED DOOR

STICK

WOOD SPACER

Warped door can be straightened by placing it under constant tension for a long period of time. Here two lengths of wire are nailed to opposite corners and tightened with a stick. The spacer provides room for twisting the stick.

The cause may also be that the door has sagged, lowering the latch bolt to a point where it can no longer enter the hole in the strike plate. If lifting the door by its handle enables the bolt to slide into place, enlarge the hole in the plate by filing its lower edge.

Another cause may be an obstruction in the doorframe that prevents the door from closing fully. Remove accumulated paint and grime from the frame and hinge surfaces.

The trouble may also be caused by displacement of the strike plate. See that the plate is in its proper position. If it is but the bolt will not enter the hole, put a little crayon on the end of the bolt so that you may see where it binds and where you need to file the strike plate to allow the bolt to enter easily.

Sticking. This is usually caused by the same conditions that prevent a door from closing, the difference being that the conditions are not as severe. Try the suggestions given previously.

If the door is stuck, make certain that the latch bolt or the dead bolt is not holding the door in place. Then take a number of butter knives and force them between the door and its frame where the pinch occurs. Next place a 2 x 4 against the inside edge of the door and tap lightly and repeatedly on the piece of wood until you drive the door open. Sandpaper the trouble spot on the door or the frame with coarse sandpaper wrapped around a block of wood.

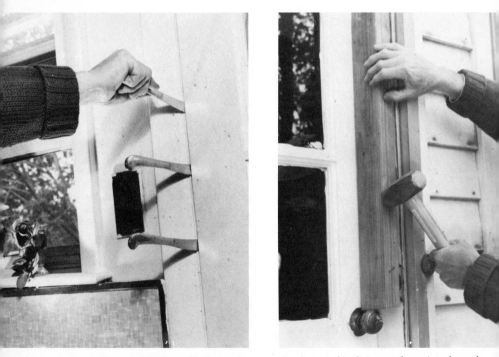

To loosen a stuck door force flat knives between the door and its frame at the point where the door sticks (left). Place a 2x4 against the other side of the door and tap gently and repeatedly on the wood with a hammer until you drive the door free of its frame (right).

DOORS, STORM

Broken frame. Use strips of plywood or metal as shown in the illustration to hold the pieces together. Use wood screws, self-tapping metal screws, or bolts to hold the strips to the doorframe.

If you do not have any of the above material, drill holes through the doorframe and tie the parts together with galvanized wire.

Broken glass. Replace the glass with a sheet of plywood, plastic, or heavy cardboard. Seal the edges of the replacement material to the storm doorframe with masking tape or Scotch tape. If the glass is only cracked, cement two strips of cardboard, one on each side of the glass, over the crack with Duco cement.

Ripped screen. If the edges of the rip have not yet been pulled apart, rejoin them with Duco or similar cement. If the edges have been separated or if there is a hole in the screen, cover the opening with a larger piece of screening. Fasten the patch in place with cement or unravel the edges of the patch and weave some of the patch wires into the screen.

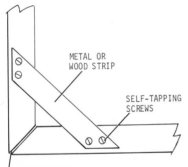

Parts of a broken storm door can be held together by using strips of plywood or metal.

As an alternative method, drill two holes through the parts of the door and hold them together with twisted wire.

One way to quickly patch a hole in a screen is to unravel the edges of a small rectangle and weave the wires into the screen.

DRAWERS, METAL

Since metal does not expand with moisture, the only cause of a stuck drawer is an obstruction. If the drawer can be moved at all, try working it backwards and forwards. That sometimes forces the obstruction out of the track. If you can't even do this, see if there is any way to disassemble the cabinet. And if there is no way of doing this you have no recourse but to force the drawer open from behind, using a flat stick as a pry bar if necessary. Once the drawer is open, look for a paper clip or a similar metal obstruction in the slides. Very old metal drawers have bearing wheels made of white metal that may have disintegrated. Sometimes you can replace them with wheels cut from plastic.

DRAWERS, WOODEN

Sticking. Most often this is caused by the parts of the cabinet and the drawer itself swelling. Remove what drawers you can from the bureau or desk. Reach up behind the stuck drawer and force it out. If you cannot do this with your hand alone use a flat stick as a pry bar to help you. Place the removed drawer in an oven turned to warm to dry it out. If possible, move the cabinet to a warm, dry room.

Sticking may also be caused by time-roughened slides. Simply rub the end of a candle over the slides to lubricate them.

Another possible cause is that the drawer bottom and the slides have worn to a point where the lower edge of a drawer strikes the top of the drawer below. The temporary cure consists of lifting the upper drawer a fraction of an inch. You can do this by forcing thumbtacks into the drawer's runners. If necessary, place small pieces of cardboard under the tacks.

Partial sticking. This is usually caused by some object either in the stuck drawer or the drawer below projecting upwards. Remove all the drawers that you can. If doing so cures the trouble, find what was projecting upwards and remove it. If the

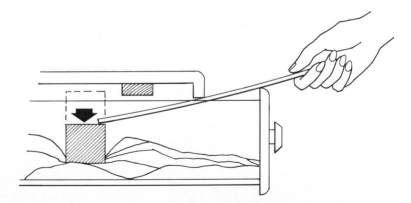

Using a ruler or flat piece of wood to lower an object that is blocking a drawer.

troublesome drawer still cannot be fully opened, use a ruler or a similar small, flat stick. Poke it gently into the drawer and push down whatever is projecting upwards. Hold the projection down with the stick and pull the drawer out.

DRIER, ELECTRIC

Won't start. Check all the fuses leading to the machine by replacing all of them at one time. If you just replace one fuse at a time and there are two bad fuses in the line, there will always be a defective fuse in the circuit and the machine, naturally, won't work.

If the fuses are good and there is power at the machine, give it 30 minutes or more to cool down. Most driers have thermostatic safety controls built into their circuits. When the machine is used continuously over a long period of time it becomes heat-soaked, and as a result the thermo safety switch opens up and stays open for a long time. This is a common complaint with old machines.

Check the safety switch in the door by leaving the door open and pushing the switch (it is a little projecting rod) in by hand. If that is the trouble, fasten a small fold of cardboard to the door with adhesive tape, positioning it so that it presses against the little rod when you close the door.

Doesn't heat up. If the machine turns but the heating coils do not get hot, try changing the temperature switch position. If that doesn't result in any heat, test all the fuses if the unit operates on 220 volts. The motors on many 220-volt driers will turn the drum even if one fuse is bad, but heat is produced only if both fuses are good.

As door buttons on electric driers wear, they must be pushed farther and farther into the machine to close the contacts. To check the button for wear, push it all the way in with the other controls in the "on" position. Then start the machine.

If the machine operates when the door button is completely depressed, fasten a piece of cardboard on the door, opposite the button, with masking tape. When the door is closed, it will now depress the button completely.

Heats but the drum doesn't rotate. If there is no sound from the machine at all, the trouble is a defective motor or the wires leading to the motor are disconnected. If you can hear the motor turn, the drive belt may have slipped off its pulley, in which case, you may be able to get it back on again and the drier working again.

Heats but doesn't dry. The cause is most likely lint blocking the air passages. Clean the lint from the screen in the front of the machine, then remove the lint from the exhaust pipe. If doing this doesn't greatly speed drying, start the machine again and place your hand over the exhaust pipe. If you feel any air movement at all the fan is working and the trouble is probably lint blocking the air passages within the machine. Disconnect the machine and turn it on its side. In some machines you can reach and clean the air passages very easily. In others, you have to disassemble a considerable portion of the works, but it isn't difficult.

If you find that air is moving out through the exhaust at a good clip and that the pipes and screen are free of lint, the trouble may not be the drier at all. You may have too many clothes in the machine and the day may be cold and damp, conditions that combined can slow drying tremendously. To speed drying under these conditions, stop the machine midway in its cycle and remove those clothes already dried. This will speed the rest of the drying.

Squeals as it turns. This means the bearings supporting the drum have worn through. The drum is rubbing against the machine's case. The sound may be horrible, but as long as the drum keeps rolling along you can continue to use it. However, the bearings and possibly the shaft should be replaced as soon as possible because if the drum gets stuck you can burn the motor out if it doesn't blow a fuse or you do not shut it off in time.

DRIER, GAS

Gas leaks. Gas is highly explosive. Always enter the laundry room with your nostrils on the alert. If there is a slight smell of gas, *leave immediately. Do not turn any lights on or off.* The smallest spark can set off an explosion. Go to the gas meter. Shut the main valve by bringing the two arms parallel to one another. Open the doors and windows leading to the drier. Wait until all of the gas smell is gone, then close the valve in the gas line leading to the drier. Next, reopen the main valve at the gas meter. If there are no leaks between the gas meter and the drier, you should smell nothing after waiting 30 minutes or more. If you do smell gas, check for leaks in the pipe by applying a mixture of soap and water to the joints. If there are bubbles, you have a leak. Do not use the drier until you have properly repaired the leak.

If there is no leak in the piping between the meter and the drier and you do not smell gas with the drier valve closed, the gas you smelled the first time was probably caused by a blown out pilot light. If you have a very old drier without an automatic pilot-light safety shutoff, the smell of gas when the pilot blows out is normal. Just make certain the air is free of gas before you follow the instructions on the side of the drier to relight the pilot. If you have a fairly new drier it probably has an automatic shutoff. This should have stopped the flow of gas as soon as its sensing element responded. In other words, when all is well with this type of machine you should never smell gas in the laundry room. If you do, it is safest to call in an expert and have it fixed.

If the smell of gas is very strong as you enter the laundry room, get your family immediately out of the house. Call for help from a neighbor's home. Do not re-enter your home under any circumstances. Let the gas utility men handle it from here.

Machine won't rotate. If the drier has been running a long time the thermo-static safety switch on the motor may have opened. Give the motor plenty of time to cool off, then try again.

If waiting doesn't produce results, check the fuses or circuit breaker. If they are satisfactory, look inside the machine. It is possible the motor is running quietly, but the belt to the drum has slipped off. In this case shut the machine off and replace the belt.

Dries very slowly. See that the valve in the gas line leading to the machine is fully open. See that lint and clothing are not clogging the filter and that the air vent is open. If the weather is cold and damp and there is an unusually large load in the drier, drying will normally take much longer than usual.

EARTHQUAKES

Preparation. Our present knowledge of earthquakes is insufficient to enable scientists to forecast their occurrence. They always arrive unexpectedly. But we do know, with fair accuracy, where earthquakes may be expected. If you live on or near a fault, the best you can do (other than move elsewhere) is to prepare yourself and your family mentally by reviewing the nature of quakes and the best courses of action to be taken during and after a quake, and by storing emergency food and gear as suggested elsewhere in this book. Most important, keep one or more small battery radios handy and in working condition. You will need them to maintain contact should the phone and power lines go down.

In itself an earthquake is no more than a pitching and shaking of the earth. No worse than a few minutes on a boat at sea. The danger of falling into a chasm opened by the quake is infinitesimal. The major danger is the possibility of being struck by falling debris or buildings, run down by unnerved motorists, or harmed by fires and explosions that may result from the earth's trembling.

Indoors. Move to the middle of the building, preferably near a central wall in the basement. If that is not possible, crawl beneath a table, bed, or sofa—anything that will provide some protection from falling objects. Do not light a cigarette or a candle. The shock may have opened a gas line. Do not go near a window or door. Prepare yourself for the aftershock. This may occur any time following the first tremors. The aftershock results from the earth wave reaching the end of its run and then returning, much like a wave on the surface of an otherwise calm pond. Your radio will probably advise you of the time element involved.

If the quake is mild, the aftershock will be equally mild. If there is little damage to the building, you can remain there, obviously. If the damage has been severe, it is best to leave as soon as you are reasonably certain you have a grace period. The aftershock may knock the structure down, especially if it is built of brick or stone.

The above assumes you are at home. If you are in a large, tall building in a major city, it is best to move quickly down to the basement or a lower floor and to remain inside until the authorities advise you it is safe to leave.

Outdoors. Move quickly away from all buildings, trees, and roads. Get out from beneath all overhead power lines. If you are on a bridge, get off as quickly as you can; at least get away from the center of the span. Remain on open ground until you are certain it is all over.

Driving an auto. Pull off the road immediately and continue going as far as you safely can. The point of this is to get out of the way of any out-of-control vehicles. Remain in the car. Turn on the radio and listen for instructions.

After the earthquake. The fact that the earth has stopped trembling means only that you and your family have survived the first danger. Everything is still far from normal and there may be as much or even more danger yet to be faced and surmounted. The first thing to do is to listen to the radio for instructions. If you have no radio, wait at least a couple of hours to make certain there are no more shocks coming and it is reasonably safe to move about.

If the building in which you and your family find yourself is a wood frame structure, and you can see no spaces between the walls or between walls and floor, if no plaster, or very little, has fallen and the chimney is still vertical, it is probably safe to remain inside providing no other dangers have arisen, such as a gas leak or an electrical fire. If you smell gas, leave immediately.

If the building you are occupying is made of brick or stone, wait until it is safe to move, then dash out the front door and keep running until you are a good distance away. The biggest danger will be when you pass through the door, because most of the loosened material will fall close to the building.

If you are outside a building, do not enter it unless it is perfectly vertical, no cracks show and nothing has fallen from the outside of the building, nor, as far as you can see, has anything broken off and fallen down inside the building. Usually, when something falls down inside an old house you can see the powdered plaster in the air.

In any event, enter gingerly and do not carry a lighted cigarette or candle with you. There may be gas, in which case the explosion that follows will be much worse than the quake.

Do not enter a flooded basement unless you can turn off the electrical power from outside the building or can reach the main switch without getting your feet in the water. With the basement flooded there is no certain way of telling in advance which pipe or appliance has become connected to the power circuit.

Do not touch any electrical appliance in your home if the appliance is wet. First, turn off the main power switch. If the appliance is soaking wet, see FLOODS, MAJOR: Restoring electrical power after the flood.

Do not leave your immediate area to see what is going on elsewhere. Roads must be kept open for emergency vehicles, and there is always the danger of falling trees and buildings. Unless you can be of assistance, stay put.

Stay clear of all fallen power lines. Phone the police or local utility company. Let them tackle the wires; they can do no harm lying on the ground. See FALLEN POWER LINES.

If you are by a stream larger than a small brook, move to higher ground. The shock may have broken a dam. Undersea quakes can send giant waves crashing up on shore hours after the tremors have passed. These giant waves will run for miles up any stream that empties into the sea.

Phone your friends and relatives. They may be worried about you and, unless they hear from you, may make the mistake of driving to help you, placing themselves in danger and interfering with rescue work.

Rest: Danger produces fear, which is highly tiring, and fear produces excitement and overexertion. There is also a natural rejoicing at having survived that results in a tremendous surge of enthusiasm and a desire to help others, right things, clean up and get going. In the young, overexertion results in a solid night's sleep; in the elderly, it can cause permanent bodily damage. This is especially true in the winter when low temperatures alone place an additional load on the heart.

Do not eat anything that has been touched by flood water; the water may be contaminated and it is much better to go hungry awhile than take a chance. Do not drink from wells that have been flooded unless you boil the water first or use purifying chemicals made for the purpose. Do not take chances eating food that may be spoiled; hunger won't hurt you, bad food will.

Keep warm: You can become seriously ill and even die if your body becomes chilled and remains so for an extended period of time. This can happen at temperatures far above freezing, so cover yourself up as soon as you feel uncomfortable. Use anything available—blankets, towels, tablecloths, even curtains.

ELECTRICAL EMERGENCIES

Fuses. A fuse has blown. You have no replacement on hand and cannot get one. Here is what you can do.

Remove a good fuse from another circuit and use it. For example, the kitchen-light fuse is burned out. You replace it temporarily with the fuse that serves the attic.

If the blown fuse is a plug fuse, remove it from the fuse block. Remove the mica window. Stuff the fuse with aluminum foil, pressed into place just as tightly as you can manage. Replace the fuse. This is a lot safer than slipping a penny behind the bad fuse. When you position the penny you make contact with a live wire. It can be your last contact with this world.

If it is a cartridge fuse that has blown and it is of the type that takes a replacement link, unscrew the ends of the fuse and use a length of thin, bare copper wire in place of the fuse link you do not have. If the cartridge ends cannot be unscrewed, drill small holes through the ends and slip a length of thin, bare copper wire through the holes. Bend the ends of the wire over the brass ends of the fuse and reinsert the fuse in its clips. In both cases the thin wire serves as the fusable link.

This fuse box combines the main fuses with the main switch. If you pull the fuse block out, you disconnect all electrical power.

The proper way to remove a cartridge fuse is to use a fuse puller. If you have no fuse puller, place one hand in your pocket, stand on a chair, and use only two fingers on the fuse.

Fluorescent lights. If a ceiling light of this type won't go on, assuming that the fuse in the circuit is good and that the bulb is known to be good, try switching the light on and off, leaving it in the on position last. Try removing the starter a few minutes after you have switched the light on. (You will have to replace the starter and remove it again every time you want to use the light.) Try turning the bulb a half turn in its socket and back again. Try placing your cigarette lighter under the starter for a minute or so.

Incandescent lights. Incandescent lamps are either all good or all bad. If they do not go on, check the fuses and try a replacement bulb. If there still isn't any light, the trouble is probably the wall switch.

Wall switches cannot be repaired, but they can be circumvented. Remove the fuse from the circuit. Remove the switch plate and the switch. Disconnect one of

Stuff the inside of a blown plug fuse with aluminum foil; it is a lot safer than placing a penny behind the bad fuse.

Replace the inside of a blown cartridge fuse with a piece of bare wire until you can secure a new fuse.

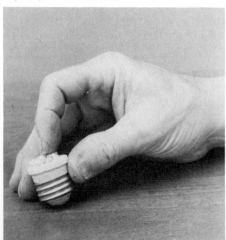

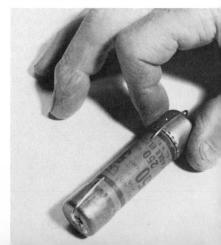

Circumvent a defective wall switch by placing both wires beneath one bolt. *Caution: Be sure to open the main switch.*

the wires and reconnect it beneath the second wire. This takes the switch out of the circuit. Replace the switch in the gem box. Replace the switch cover and then the fuse. To turn your ceiling light off you will have to unscrew the light bulb or remove the fuse. This is a nuisance, but at least you have light.

Table lamps. The most common source of trouble is to be found at the plug. Examine it and if it is of the molded type, try pulling sideways on the wire. If the wires are loose you can usually pull them out. If this is the case, replace the plug.

The next most common trouble is the socket switch. Try tightening the light bulb and working the switch. If that doesn't help, try loosening the bulb half a turn and then test the switch. Sometimes the switch will work only when the bulb is relatively loose in the socket.

Sparks and shocks when the lamp is touched are usually caused by lack of insulation on the electrical cord at the point where it enters the bottom of the lamp. Remove the lamp's plug from the wall and with adhesive or other tape, reinsulate the wires.

Molded-in-place plug can be tested by pulling sideways on its wires.

Convert a table lamp to an extension cord by removing the shade and bulb and putting a screw-in receptacle in its place.

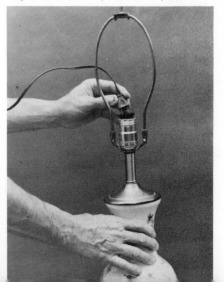

Temporary extension cord. Remove the shade and light bulb from a table lamp. Replace the lamp with a screw-plug receptacle. Now you can use the lamp as an electrical extension cord.

Temporary splice. To join the ends of two electrical cords when you do not have the necessary tools to solder and insulate the joints properly, stagger the ends of the wire pairs so that each joint is 2 inches or so from its neighbor. When you do this you can insulate the joints with masking tape, Scotch tape, or even dry paper held in place with a string with little danger that there will be a short. Obviously, the splice must be made properly as soon as possible.

Emergency lights. Obviously it is wise to always have at least one flashlight in working condition at home in a convenient location known to all. Not so obvious, perhaps, is the fact that votive candles—the type that are molded inside a glass—will give you many more hours of light than even the best alkaline dry cell. Therefore a number of these candles should also be kept on hand as a guard against darkness in addition to a flashlight. A votive candle will usually burn upwards of 24 hours.

Votive candles are much better than ordinary candles as emergency lights because they cannot be easily blown out by a wind. To fasten an ordinary candle within a glass, attach the bottom of the candle to a small circle of cardboard with a drop of hot wax or a tack. Then place the candle on its base inside the glass.

A lamp can be fashioned from a saucer, a strip of cloth, a piece of cork, and any kind of oil you may have on hand, including cooking oil and barbecue lighting fluid. (Alcohol burns almost without light and gasoline is much too dangerous.)

A large votive candle such as this one will provide continuous light for many days. The flashlight won't provide more than a few hours at best.

To convert an ordinary candle to a storm candle, fasten a disc of cardboard to the bottom. If you put the candle in a measuring cup, you will have a hurricane lamp with a handle.

A small strip of cotton pulled through a hole in a section of cork makes a floating wick for this simple oil lamp.

Fill the saucer half full of oil. Make a hole in the piece of cork. Slide the strip of cloth through the hole so that about ½ inch of cloth extends beyond the cork. Place the cork on the oil with the short end of the cloth projecting upwards. Wait a moment until the cloth, which is now a wick, absorbs oil and then light it. You now have a one-candle power lamp, smoky but effective.

If you don't have a piece of cork you can use a paper clip to hold the wick to the side of the saucer. The lamp works just as well this way but you have to keep lowering the wick (or adding oil) as the level of the oil drops.

FALLEN POWER LINES

You cannot tell if the fallen line is carrying current or not just by looking at it and you cannot test it for power by any safe means at your disposal. Remember, the mere fact that there are no sparks flying simply means the power line is not on television or in the movies. It doesn't mean the line is dead. (Actually, it only means that the earth is fairly dry.) Therefore, never approach a fallen power line unless it is a matter of life or death and then approach it only with the greatest caution.

If a power line has fallen on an individual and he is mobile, have him slide out from underneath without touching the wire or wires. If he cannot do this, have him remain still while you phone for help. If it is obvious that he must be moved immediately, use a long, dry 2 x 4 or a wooden broom handle and lift the wire slowly and carefully, while someone else pulls the man to one side. Then when you have lowered the wire back onto the earth, and the man is a good distance away, you can attend to him.

Meanwhile, have barriers and flares set up to keep others away from the fallen power lines.

FALLEN TREES

Fallen trees and similar heavy objects beyond your bare-hand strength can always be moved and even raised with mechanical help. The trick is to contrive to use whatever aids you may have on hand to do the job.

Using an automobile. A tree that has fallen across your driveway, trapping your car, can be pushed out of the way. Cut whatever branches may be necessary to permit you to rest your car's bumper against the trunk of the tree. Then cut off any branches on the other side of the tree that appear as though they will dig into the earth when the tree moves. Put the car in its lowest forward gear and push as gently as you can manage. If you cannot move the tree, do not back off and ram it (this will wreck your car) but try placing some skid boards under it as described a little farther on.

To pull a tree or any other heavy object with your car, bring the front of the car close to the tree. Tie the tree to the car's bumper, taking care to position the rope near the bumper support and to place a small board between the edge of the metal and the rope, otherwise the metal will cut through the rope. If you can't fit the rope behind the bumper, tie it around the frame of the car. Loop the rope as many times as you can between the car and the tree. (Remember, ½-inch-thick Manila rope is good for only about 1,000 pounds—steady pull.) This done, cut off the tree limbs that may get in the way. Back the car very slowly away from the tree until the slack in the rope is taken up, then try pulling the tree. The car is placed in this position because every car's reverse gear is slower than its lowest forward gear, and the slower the gear the more pull or push you have.

Moving a tree without a car. Cut off any branches that have penetrated the earth or are bent against the earth, pointing in the direction you wish to move the tree. These branches will dig in when the tree is moved and thereby stop you.

If the trunk of the tree is no more than a foot in diameter, cut a sharp point on the end of a 2 x 4 and use it as a lever to pry the tree in the direction you wish. If you have a piece of 1¼-inch pipe 6 feet long or more, flatten one end and use that as a lever.

If you have an auto jack, place it beneath a branch that projects horizontally from the side of the tree opposite to the direction in which you wish to move the tree. Operate the jack and elevate the tree a few inches. Then stand clear of the jack and push the tree off the jack in the desired direction. Doing all this will give you a couple of inches. Just repeat the operation again and again until you have moved the tree as far as you need to. But remember to stay clear of the jack. The tree may kick it out as it falls.

If you have enough rope and there is a strong tree nearby, loop the rope around the standing tree and the fallen tree trunk half a dozen or more times. Pull the rope snug and then wrap the ends around the tree trunks and tie them. Next, slip a 2 x 4 between the ropes and by revolving the piece of lumber around the ropes, twist them. This will exert a tremendous pressure on the two trees. Hopefully, the fallen tree will move. When you have twisted the ropes as much as you can, remove the 2 x 4, untie the rope and take up the slack. Then retie the rope and repeat the twisting operation.

If you have no rope, drive two 2 x 4s or 4 x 4s into the earth tightly alongside the fallen tree. Then drive wedges between the 2 x 4s and the tree trunk. This

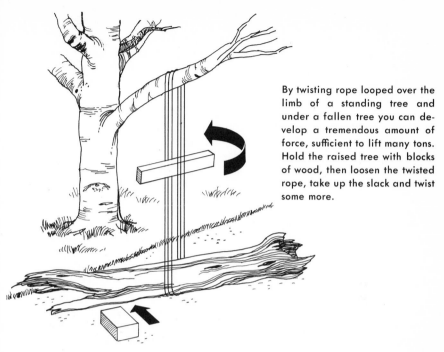

By twisting rope looped over the limb of a standing tree and under a fallen tree you can develop a tremendous amount of force, sufficient to lift many tons. Hold the raised tree with blocks of wood, then loosen the twisted rope, take up the slack and twist some more.

will move the trunk (providing the 2 x 4s don't give). Place wood spacers between the 2 x 4s and the tree trunk and use the wedges again. To facilitate the side movement of the tree trunk, taper the ends of two 2 x 4s and drive them under the tree. They will lift the trunk a fraction of an inch and act as runners on which the tree can slide more easily than on the soil.

To lift a tree. Drive a pair of 2 x 6s or large planks, side by side, under the fallen tree trunk. Place a wedge on one plank and drive it between the plank and the tree trunk. Then place a second wedge on the same plank on the opposite side of the trunk. Drive the two wedges toward each other until you have lifted the tree trunk an inch or more. Then slide a 1-inch board between the second plank and the tree trunk. Next, place two facing wedges on top of the board, beneath the tree trunk, and drive them toward each other. This will release the first pair of wedges, and when the trunk is high enough you will be able to place a 2-inch-thick spacer on top of the first plank. By repeating these operations again and again you can lift a tree trunk several feet into the air.

If the fallen tree is beneath a strong limb of another tree and you have sufficient rope, you can use the rope-twisting trick previously described to lift the fallen tree. You will of course require spacers to hold the raised trunk up while you take up the slack in the rope.

You can also lift a fallen tree with an automotive scissor jack. However, to get it under the tree trunk you may have to dig a small trench beneath the tree. Ordinary auto jacks can also be used but only if you have two of them. You need one on each side of the tree to hold the tree in place. Do not depend on these jacks or the scissor jack holding the trunk up for any length of time. Keep building increasingly higher block supports beneath the tree as you raise it.

FAN, ATTIC

Fan operates, but there is little air movement. See that the louvers (if there are any) in line with the fan are open. Check that the rooms from which the fan is drawing air have open windows. If the fan slows down a bit and its tone deepens when you open a window, you will know that is the cause of the difficulty. Fans always run more rapidly when their air flow is blocked.

If the problem is not caused by closed windows, shut the fan off and try spinning the fan blade by hand. If the fan does not spin freely, try a few drops of light motor oil on the bearings. If that doesn't loosen the bearings, try a few drops of Liquid Wrench. Follow this with a few drops of motor oil and try spinning the fan blades one more time. If the fan's shaft is still tight in its bearings, try tightening the motor frame bolts. When these bolts are very loose, the bearings sometimes bind the shaft.

Doesn't shut off. If the fan switch is temperature-controlled, it is possible the temperature hasn't dropped down far enough although you may feel cool. Adjust the switch to shut off at a slightly higher temperature. If it shuts the fan off when you do this, you know the switch is functioning properly. If it doesn't shut the fan off, your only practical alternative at this time is to operate the attic fan switch by hand. There is also the possibility that something has been placed over the thermostatic switch, insulating it. In such cases the switch would not respond until the temperature has dropped far below its setting. The cure, of course, is to remove the insulating material.

Noisy. Shut the fan off and inspect the setscrew holding the fan to the shaft. Tighten it if it is loose. Check that the louvers are not loose. Combined with a varying wind loose louvers can cause a lot of noise. Still another possible cause of noise is paper or leaves or even loose insulation in the fan's air path. Since this material rattles and pings when the fan is running it sounds as though the fan is making the noise. Although this loose material causes no harm, the noise is annoying and so the air path must be cleared.

Won't start. If the fan doesn't start as soon as the switch is thrown, turn the switch off. Then check the fan fuse or circuit breaker. If it is satisfactory, try the switch again. If there is still no operation, turn the switch off quickly and inspect the fan. Look for obstructions such as an unfortunate bird or mouse or even paper that has become entangled with the fan blades. If this is not the trouble, remove the fan's fuse or open the circuit breaker. Then open the metal box in which the fan's wires are connected to the house wires. See that the wire nuts on connecting wires are all tight.

FAN, KITCHEN OR WINDOW

Noisy. Remove the fan's plug from the wall outlet. Inspect the fan for a loose wire cage. See that the fan is tight on the motor shaft. Check that the fan blades have not been bent. If they have, straighten them carefully.

Sparks. Sparks emanating from the line cord where it enters the fan motor housing are caused by the use of cooking oil as a bearing lubricant. Oil has dripped down and dissolved the rubber. Replace the line cord, or separate the bare wires and wrap each of them with adhesive tape. Continue using the fan in this state only as long as is necessary to secure a new line cord.

Excessive sparks emanating from inside the motor may be caused by worn brushes or softened brush springs. Remove the fan's plug from the wall outlet. Unscrew the little plastic cap that holds one motor brush in place. Remove the brush and its spring. Expand the spring a little by pulling on it. Replace the brush and spring. Do the same to the other brush and spring. Expanding the spring usually produces a better contact between the brush and the commutator for a little while. For a permanent repair the brushes and their springs should be replaced. Note that a thin ring of sparks around the commutator is normal with this type of motor.

Won't start. If the motor is silent, check the wall outlet for electrical power by plugging a properly functioning light into the outlet. If there is power, inspect the fan's plug. If it is a molded plug, try pulling the wire sideways out of the plug. Properly fastened wires cannot be pulled out of the plug. If the plug is not at fault, inspect the other end of the line cord. See that the wires at that end are properly connected. If all the wires appear to be satisfactory, plug the fan in and carefully give the fan blades a little push. If the fan turns and comes up to its proper speed, the cause of the difficulty may be that the brushes are loose or stuck in their passages. Try following the procedure for expanding the brush springs just described. If the fan runs poorly after being started by hand, the trouble is probably due to an open winding. There is nothing you can do at this time beyond running it as it is. Later, you can replace the armature or the entire unit.

If the motor hums but won't turn over, remove the plug and try spinning the blades by hand. If the fan is difficult to turn, the trouble is probably caused by the use of cooking oil in place of motor oil as a lubricant. Cooking oil turns into a kind of glue when it is heated. The cure is to either disassemble the motor and clean the bearings and oil cups, if there are any, and lubricate with light machine oil, or try a few drops of Liquid Wrench or any similar type of solvent and follow this with a few drops of motor oil.

Place a fan on a flat surface if you want to see whether or not its blades are properly aligned.

If, on the other hand, the fan is easily spun when the power is off but just hums to itself with the power on, the chances are that the armature or stator is loose and one is pulled against the other when power is turned on. Check the motor bolts (the long bolts that run through the motor). If they are loose, tighten them. If they are tight, loosen them. These tricks sometimes work when the motor shaft is slightly bent.

Vibrates badly. Vibration is usually caused by either a loose or a bent fan. First, make certain the fan is tight on its shaft. If that isn't the trouble, remove the fan from its shaft and place it on a flat surface. This will help you find the bent blade. Straighten it and replace the fan on its shaft.

FAUCET

Drips from handle. This is caused by water leaking past the packing around the spindle. First, try tightening the cap nut (the large nut under the handle). If that doesn't stop the leak, shut the water off by either closing the valve in the pipe line connected directly to the faucet or the main valve. Back the cap nut off. (You may have to remove the handle on some faucets.) Wrap string that has been rubbed in wax around the spindle. Replace the cap nut and tighten it until the water stops leaking out.

Drips from spout. Close the valve in the line leading to the faucet. Disassemble the faucet and remove the spindle. Remove the old washer on the bottom of the

Waxed string can be used as packing around a faucet stem to stop a leak.

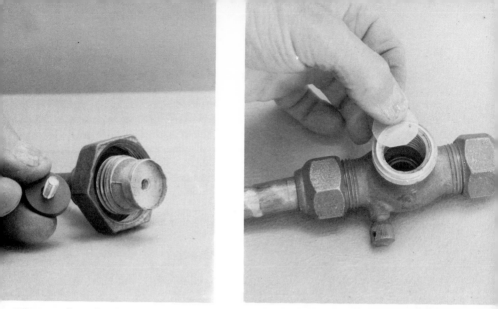

When you do not have a replacement washer (left), turn the old one and use it again. When the old washer is too badly mangled to be turned over and you must stop the flow of the water through a faucet or valve, place a disc of rubber or soft plastic on the valve seat (right). When the stem is screwed in place, the flow will be stopped.

spindle. If you have a replacement washer, install it. If not, turn the old washer over and reassemble the faucet. If the old washer has disintegrated, you can cut a new washer from a piece of rubber. If you don't want to go to the trouble, place a piece of rubber over the opening in the bottom of the faucet and then reassemble it. When you turn the spindle to the closed position, you will stop the flow of water, but you will not be able to open and close the faucet as you normally would. The value of this arrangement is that you can now open the valve leading to the defective faucet without it dripping or running.

Handle loose. Remove the handle. With the point of a knife clean the splines in the handle and the spindle. Reassemble. If the handle is still loose, file a little off the top of the spindle. This will force the handle more tightly against the spindle. Another method of making a handle tight on a faucet spindle consists of enlarging one of the spline grooves in the spindle with a hacksaw. A short piece of bare copper wire is fitted into the saw groove. When the handle is forced over the wire and the spindle, the wire holds the faucet tightly in place.

FIRE: GENERAL RECOMMENDATIONS

As in the case of almost all other emergencies, the greatest danger during a fire is usually ourselves. It is human nature to freeze or flee when frightened, and the roar of flames and the smell of smoke are as frightening as anything we may encounter. Survival, however, almost never lies in either of these extreme actions. If you do not move there is an excellent chance you will perish, and if you run wildly about, your chances of survival aren't much better.

45

But to characterize fear as an overresponse is wrong. Fire and smoke do kill. The temperature in a burning building will vary from 400 to 1,000° F. Human hair singes at just 158° F. Breathe air at 300° F for just one minute and you are dead. A 1,000° F temperature on one floor can cause bedclothes, curtains, books, and even furniture on the floor above to explode into flames. It isn't necessary for a flame to actually touch something to set it afire; the radiated heat can do it. And the heat itself is not the major cause of death. Many more people have been killed by smoke poisoning and attendant asphyxiation. Smoke is composed of a dozen dangerous gases, including hydrogen sulfide, ammonia, hydrocyanic acid, phosgene, and carbon monoxide. Inhale the latter a few times and you will be rendered unconscious. Continuous breathing of the gas will kill you in less than 3 minutes. Incidentally, the white smoke with the beautiful smell that emanates from a wood fire is deadly poisonous. Carbon monoxide, of course, has no odor whatsoever.

Our instinctive dread of fire is therefore well-founded. But there is no reason to panic. Fire can be prevented and circumvented. It does not race down hallways and through buildings with the speed of a bullet. It is stopped for 20 to 30 minutes by flammable barriers such as wood doors. And there is almost always 2 inches of pure air next to the floor in any smoke-filled room.

Prevention. Make it your practice to check all kitchen "fires" before going to bed; to drench the fire in your fireplace when you go to bed or leave your home; never to leave small children alone at home nor to let them play in the kitchen near the stove; to keep the basement and cellar free of papers and trash; to keep flammable material yards away from a furnace; never to use worn and frayed appliance cords, nor to plug so many cords into one outlet that your floor looks like a vine-covered jungle; never to store gasoline or other easily ignited materials in your home or garage; never to smoke while drinking heavily and never to smoke in bed.

Support these safety measures by installing several automatic, battery-operated smoke alarms in your home. These devices sound a warning as soon as smoke reaches them. They can save your life and your family's lives. Keep a fire extinguisher or two in your home. The first should go in the kitchen. The second should go in the basement just outside the furnace room, or if there is no partition sepa-

Small B/C extinguisher suitable for home use. Dial on top indicates contents.

rating the furnace from the rest of the cellar, the second extinguisher should be positioned several yards away. The best is a Class B/C extinguisher. It can be used against all fires. A Class B extinguisher can be used on Class A fires; wood, paper, fabric, and Class B fires; flammable liquids. A Class B/C or C extinguisher can also be used on electrical fires. The others cannot.

Fire drill. Prepare yourself and your family now for the possibility of a fire. Drill your family in their respective duties. Do this every few months at night and make certain they all go through the necessary steps. Plan and rehearse what you will do if the stairs are burning; if the fire is in the front of the house or the rear of the house. Decide who will help the young and the aged. Show them how to bend low to find air; how to cover their faces with a wet cloth to reduce fumes. (This does not eliminate poisonous gases.) Make certain everyone knows and understands the nature of fire and the self-protective steps they can take, as discussed in the following sections.

Decide on where you will meet outdoors, on who is going to run to the firebox and who is going to run to a neighbor's house to phone the alarm. Not only will these drills greatly reduce the possibility of calamity in your home, but if you or other members of your family are caught in a fire elsewhere this knowledge and experience will help everyone.

Extinguishing a fire. Bear in mind that the wrong action in fighting a fire is worse than doing nothing at all. For example, if you pour water or apply a Class A extinguisher to a fire containing oil and/or grease you will spread the fire. If you direct water or a stream from a Class A extinguisher on an electrical fire—a fire which contains live electrical wires—you can electrocute yourself. On the other hand, if you recognize your fallibility and rush for help, the minutes you save can mean the difference between the firemen winning or losing their battle with the fire. There is no doubt in anyone's mind that the first few minutes are most crucial in fighting a fire.

Let us assume that you have the correct fire-fighting equipment: water or any extinguisher for a fire involving paper, wood, and similar substances; a Class B or better extinguisher for any fire involving oil or gasoline or grease; a Class B/C or C extinguisher for any fire including a fire involving live electrical wires.

Play the stream on the base of the fire. Your intent should be to wet or smother the material that is burning. Spraying water or chemicals into the flames achieves nothing except to cool the fire a bit.

As you fight the fire, examine the area around the fire. Try to foresee the path the fire will take. If it is safe, have someone take flammable objects out of the fire's path. If there is a wind, stop fighting and run. If the fire is approaching highly volatile material, quit and run.

While you are fighting the fire, send someone for help. Have them call the fire alarm in or use the nearest firebox or do both. When the firebox is used the individual using it should remain there to direct the firemen to your home.

Should you manage to extinguish the flames, keep pouring water or extinguisher chemicals on the burned material. It must be thoroughly soaked to make certain the fire will not rekindle itself. Such items as pillows, mattresses, and soft furniture should be dragged out and clear of the building. It is not unusual for a spark to remain alive within a mattress for days and burn fiercely again when a wind comes up.

FIRES, AUTOMOBILE

On the road. Very often an automotive fire is preceded by abnormal operation. The engine is sluggish, you can hear the sound of frying or smell hot oil. Sometimes smoke may be visible when you stop for a light. In any case, if there is any suspicion that the car is on fire, slow down immediately and pull well off the road. Then just run out of the car and examine it from a distance. If it is obvious that the car is on fire, give it 50 yards of clearance and call for help.

While it is wise to carry a fire extinguisher in your car, positioned within easy reach, it is foolish to risk your life trying to put out an automotive fire when nothing more than a vehicle is at stake. Automotive fires are unpredictable. Although the fire may obviously be confined to the engine compartment, you have no way of knowing whether or not the rubber gasoline feed pipe has opened. If it has or when it does there may be an explosion. Just carry fire insurance and let it burn. The time to use your extinguisher is only when there is a life at stake; auto fires are that dangerous.

In the garage. If there is just the smell of fire and very little smoke, drive the car out of the garage and away from the house. Do not race the engine, for the fan will feed the fire more air. Shut the engine off. Call for help. Do not hesitate. The fire department would rather respond to an honest mistake (if there is no fire) than come to your house after the car is in flames and possibly has exploded, setting nearby property afire.

Upholstery fire. If a lit cigarette or match has fallen unnoticed onto the upholstery and slowly burned its way inside before you discover the fire, do not merely soak the burned area. *Remove the seat.* It is difficult to extinguish an upholstery fire completely. (This is also true of household furniture.) It is not unusual for a fire of this kind to blaze up days later after having been thoroughly soaked with water. So place the burned seat (or chair) on your driveway, clear of everything else and let it sit there a few days, at least, while you observe it.

FIRES, ELECTRICAL

Appliances. Under certain conditions, the roast or some other dish you have cooking in your electric oven will catch on fire. When this happens, shut the oven off and leave the door closed for at least 30 minutes. If the fire rekindles itself when you open the oven, close the door for another 30 minutes. The lack of oxygen will smother the fire, and with time the inside of the oven will cool to below the oil's burning temperature.

When a toaster or some similar device catches fire, pull its cord out of the wall. Then, smother the flames with a wet towel or a similar material. *Do not throw water on the appliance while it is still plugged in.* You can douse it with water after you have pulled its plug, but *not before.* Switching the device off does not necessarily keep you from electrocuting yourself should you throw water on the appliance with its plug still in the wall outlet.

Equipment. When a piece of permanently connected electrical equipment catches fire, shut it off. If you have a Class B/C or C extinguisher on hand, use it. If you have nothing but water or a Class A or B extinguisher, there is nothing you can safely do to quench the fire without first pulling the main fuses or opening the main switch. When either or both of these two measures have been taken, you can soak the equipment with water or any fire-fighting solution. If, however, the fire is not limited to the equipment but has spread beyond, take your family and run.

If an oil burner has caught on fire, throw the safety switch at the head of the stairs. (There is also a shutoff switch at the side of the furnace.) If you can see no flames, close the valves in the oil lines leading to the burner. If the burner is inside the metal furnace cover, as is usually the case, there is little danger in letting the fire burn itself out. However, you should call the fire department immediately just to be safe. If you can see flames from the head of the stairs, just open the safety switch and leave with your family.

Fixtures. When smoke issues from behind a ceiling or wall fixture or you can see or hear sparks, the cause is almost always water. Somehow water from a leaky pipe or a leak in the roof has gotten into the fixture and is causing a partial short circuit. Switch the fixture off. Pull the main fuse or open the main switch. Then lower the fixture and find the source and stop the flow of water into the fixture. In most cases your best move is to replace or at least rewire the fixture. Just drying it doesn't remove the carbonized insulation, which will now conduct electricity, wet or dry.

Wires. When the insulation has been worn away on an appliance cord and two bare wires touch, the resultant short circuit will cause a fire if it doesn't blow the fuse first. When the fire is still in the spark stage you can simply pull the plug out. When you cannot touch the plug, pull the entire appliance away from the wall and remove the plug this way.

Water within the walls of a building or a nail accidentally driven into a cable can cause a short circuit which in turn can cause a fire. When this happens and you have time, pull the main switch and leave. Do not remain inside the building as there is no way of knowing how long the fire has been burning and how extensive it may be within the walls, floors, and ceilings. Call the fire department and let them open the walls and put the fire out.

FIRES, HOUSE

In the preceding sections we have discussed the measures to be taken in the event of a specific, limited fire. The directions following apply to fires that involve or appear to involve the building.

Obviously, the prime consideration is to make certain everyone leaves the building just as quickly as possible. Equally obvious is the fact that it is not enough to appoint yourself fire warden and take on the responsibility of rousing everyone and herding them outside. You may be trapped in your room; you may be injured;

hallways may become impassable. The only sensible arrangement is to appoint each and every individual in your home a fire warden and train them all in what they must do in the event of a fire. For further details on fire drill see FIRE, GENERAL RECOMMENDATIONS.

Escape routes. As an antifire precaution, have everyone sleep with the bedroom door closed. On being awakened by the sound of the family dog, the smell of smoke, or a smoke alarm bell ringing, no one is to rush out of the door. They may be met by a wall of flame. Instead, they should try the doorknob. If it isn't hot, they are to hold their breath and open the door a fraction of an inch. If there is no fire in the hall, they are to rush out to warn the others after closing the door behind themselves.

If flames bar the exit through the door, they are to close the door and stuff pillows and clothing near its bottom to keep the gases out. As stated, a wooden door can keep a fire out of a room for 20 to 30 minutes. This fact must be impressed upon everyone. They must know there is no need to panic; that there is plenty of time to wait for help and to help themselves. During this time they should open the window and attract attention by shouting and throwing things out. At the same time they should bang on the walls to awaken others who may be sleeping nearby. They should also prepare for leaving the room by the window by making a rope from bed sheets and blankets; even clothing may be used. They should further ensure a safe landing by throwing pillows and mattresses down on the ground.

And most important, if the room is more than a dozen feet up, they are not to slide down their makeshift rope until the very last minute. There is no way of knowing without testing whether the makeshift rope will hold or not, and remember, a 40-foot fall onto concrete is certain death. (If there is a bedroom in your home that is more than 20 feet above the ground it is advisable to store a rope escape ladder there and to have the children practice using it from time to time.)

Dashing through flames. Although no one should enter a burning building for any reason whatsoever because it is almost certain death, there may be times when it is necessary and even advisable to dash down a smoke-filled hallway. Should this be necessary, protect yourself by putting on shoes, a heavy overcoat, and a hat, preferably of the type that can be pulled well down over the ears. Wet a towel or piece of cloth and hold it over your face. The cloth will filter out the dust particles that will make you cough and choke, but not the poisonous fumes.

Take a number of deep breaths to load up on oxygen, then go quickly to your destination, holding your breath when you pass through smoke. When it is necessary to breathe, bend close to the floor. If there is any pure air in the room at all you will find it there. Do not sprint because to do so uses too much oxygen.

Clothing on fire. If a removable piece of your clothing catches on fire, take it off. If it is burning too strongly for that, lie down on the floor with your arms up over your face and roll slowly over and over. If possible, roll yourself up in a rug, a blanket, or anything else that can smother the fire.

If someone else's clothing is on fire, stop them from running. To run with one's clothing on fire is to become a human torch and die. Force the individual to the floor and roll them over and over to smother the flames. If possible, have someone bring a blanket or rug and wrap it around the victim.

FIRES, KITCHEN

Pot fires. Turn off the fire under the pot and cover the pot with a close-fitting lid. Then just wait. Don't throw water on the pot; the heat may cause the water to turn instantly into steam and explode in your face.

If an oil-filled pan has caught fire, do not attempt to move it. You may spill burning oil on yourself or the floor. Do not throw water on the fire. The water will spread the oil and the fire. Use a Class B, B/C, or C extinguisher with great care. Although any of these extinguishers can be used on an oil fire, if you spray the chemicals too vigorously you will possibly blow the oil out of the pan and so spread the fire. If you have a large metal pan or pot cover, place it carefully over the flames, using an oven glove to hold it. Then back away and remain there until the fire goes out.

Gas-oven fires. Gas ovens are always open to the air so it is impossible to smother a gas-oven fire the way you can smother an electric-oven fire. The best you can do is turn the gas off and watch the fire a second. If it appears that the flames will confine themselves to the oven, wait the fire out. If it seems that the flames may reach out beyond the oven, remove everything flammable nearby, then fight the flames with a Class B, B/C, or C extinguisher. If you have no extinguisher, and if the flames are strong and hungry, get everyone out of the house and go for help.

For electric-oven fires, see FIRES, ELECTRICAL: Appliances.

FLOODS, MAJOR

The areas that have been flooded in the past and which may be flooded in the future are well known. Generally, the advent of a flood is known for several hours and even days in advance. Unless it is a dam that gives way suddenly, there is little chance you will be caught by surprise if you make it your business to keep abreast of local news. However, the warning may not be of much help if you are not prepared to act immediately.

Since it is almost always best to leave the area as quickly as possible, not only must you and your family be ready to leave on short notice, you must have transportation, a destination, and a home that you can leave with a minimum of loss.

The ideal home in flood country is a tethered ark. The next best is a home constructed on a slab that has a number of holes through it so that water cannot collect underneath and lift the slab and house.

In an existing home the best you can do is to avoid investing in expensive furniture, refinishing the basement, and otherwise improving a home that may have to be abandoned to floodwater. It is also wise to make it your practice not to keep valuables such as antiques, paintings, and jewels at home. In flood country there is always the chance you'll have barely enough time to collect the children and pets and flee. Anything that is going to make you hesitate to run should be avoided.

Financial preparation. Take out flood insurance, if a company will issue it, for your home. Prepare a line of credit at a local bank and a bank close by your proposed destination in case of floods. In this way you can be certain of having the money necessary to tide you over without going to a strange bank in a strange city for the first time and waiting in line with other flood victims trying to borrow money. The very fact that you have had the foresight to prepare for a financial emergency will earn you a few points with the banker you deal with.

Transportation. Make it your business to keep your car in good condition and full of gas. To be certain you will always have sufficient gas, store a 5-gallon can on the grounds. *Do not keep it in the car or indoors.* Don't put off fixing the spare tire or buying new tires. Keep in the car the tools and other equipment that were suggested in the section on AUTOMOBILES. And even though you know you have only a short distance to go to safety, always keep a supply of nonperishable food and water in your car. You never know what may prevent you from reaching your destination quickly, and you can't drink floodwater. It can make you sick. In cold weather store blankets and extra outer clothes in a plastic bag in the car. The plastic will keep the clothing dry.

Destination. Prepare your destination well in advance. If you can't double up with a relative or friend in a safe area, inquire of the local Red Cross as to where you will be directed in an emergency. Find out what you are expected to bring along. Ask if they have an alternate relief station in case the nearest station becomes inaccessible or overcrowded. If you have no relief station and no friends to go to, locate a safe, high, dry area where you and your family can camp out for awhile. In such cases, of course, you will have to store camping gear and food near your car for a quick getaway.

Before leaving. Shut the main gas valve at the gas meter. Open the power switch and remove the main fuses. If you have plenty of time, take whatever is of value to an upper floor. Seal the cellar floor drain, the toilets, and the drains in the sinks with newspapers. This will keep the mud out of your drain system. Place large plastic bags in which you have made a few small holes over your electrical equipment. Tie the bags in place. The bags won't keep the equipment dry, but they will greatly reduce the mud that might otherwise enter.

This main gas valve is in open position. To close it the two arms must be brought parallel to one another (holes in line). The necessary wrench, which is kept on the valve, has been removed for the photograph.

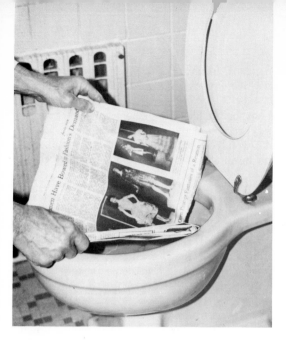

If you are expecting a major flood, close off the toilet, sinks, and cellar floor drains with newspaper to keep the mud out.

Open the cellar doors and windows. Do not build an earth or sandbag dam around the house. You don't want water piling up against the dam and then breaking through it to slam against the house, neither do you want water rising up outside an empty cellar. In both cases the water can smash the foundation walls and completely ruin the building. With water inside the building the pressure on the foundation walls is minimized.

If there are any animals that you cannot take with you, turn them loose. They can swim and, free, they may be able to save themselves.

Driving. Take the routes advised by the authorities. Don't take short cuts or leave the main highways if you can possibly help it. Don't drive through any body of water without first checking its depth. Stop the car and wade. It is better to have wet feet than to find the road dips down below the top of your hood.

Go slowly when driving through water but keep your engine revs high. Moving slowly through the water will reduce the possibility of splashing water up on the ignition. Keeping engine revs high will help keep the engine going should some of the wires get wet. You can do this on an automatic by holding your foot lightly on the brake while you give it the gas. On a stick-shift car, shift to first gear. If the motor gets wet, put it in neutral and keep revving it until it stops missing. Then proceed.

Restoring electrical power after the flood. Do not rush into your home and throw the main switch without first examining everything electrical. Bear in mind that clean water will not harm electrical equipment—even radios and hi-fi equipment (except for speakers), if following the inundation the equipment is made *perfectly* dry before it is used again.

The reason is that damp or moist insulation will pass electrical current which will carbonize the insulation. Since carbon is a conductor, the condition becomes worse with time. The more current that flows through the insulation, the more the insulation conducts until finally you have an electrical fire.

If your home has been flooded with salt water, you must wash everything thoroughly with clean, fresh water and then dry it perfectly before attempting to use it.

To speed drying, take everything apart. Remove the wall switch and wall outlet covers, drop the ceiling lights; take the appliances apart and bring the parts out into the sun.

On the other hand, if the flood has merely filled the bottom few inches of your basement with water and hasn't reached any of the electrical equipment, you can turn the power on immediately, after you have taken the trouble to stand on a dry chair. Standing in water when you throw the switch or replace the main fuse is inviting electrocution.

Cleaning up. Go to it with a system or you will be wasting most of your effort. Start by carrying everything soiled out of the building. A little rain cannot do any of it much harm now. Make a pile of all the material that cannot be returned to use. Do not include such things as rugs and sheets and clothing. Mud can be washed off. But do include soft furniture and the like. Move the discard pile a goodly distance away to keep up your morale. Use a garden hose to clean that which you believe can be returned to service, but don't bring any of it inside until it is at least mud-free.

Meanwhile, have the rest of your crew get to work cleaning the house. Let them start above the flood level and work downwards. In this way there will be a minimum of mud tracked into the cleaned portions of the building. Do not attempt to clean everything perfectly at first. Just remove the mud. Later, when everything has settled down, you can clean as much as necessary. First, you need a home you can live in again.

As stated in regard to EARTHQUAKES, the excitement of merely surviving leads to overexertion that can be much more damaging than the flood. Make up your mind that it was an act of God and that there is no reason why everything has to be brought back to its original condition in a day. If you, your family, and home have survived the flood, there is no reason to doubt that you can survive a few days of mud and confusion. In other words, don't kill yourself cleaning up after you have escaped drowning.

FLOODS, MINOR

Use whatever means you have at hand to prevent the water from entering your cellar or basement. If you can, make a small embankment of earth in front of the cellar door. Use concrete block, bricks, or even planks to make a wall if you have no soil. Anything that reduces the flow of water into your cellar will reduce the damage and the work necessary to remove the water.

For water removal, rent a portable pump, if you can. Phone the fire department. In some towns the fire fighters will pump your cellar out for free in an emergency. If there is a house drain clean-out in the cellar floor, open the drain by removing the plug and rid yourself of the water that way. If there is nothing else, form a bucket brigade and empty the cellar by hand. A few hours more or less don't matter, but the sooner you drain the cellar the less damage the water will do to the timbers and flooring that may be there.

To speed drying, open all the windows and the doors. Turn the heat up and place a ventilating fan in one of the windows.

FREEZER, REFRIGERATOR

Both these pieces of equipment operate in an identical manner and have therefore been included under the same head.

Insufficiently cold. The unit is old and has lost efficiency. All you can do other than recharge the unit or overhaul it is help it along by moving it away from the wall so that the air circulates more freely over its coils, or possibly moving it to a cooler place in your home.

Doesn't run. Obviously the first thing to check is the outlet to make certain power is reaching the unit. Then check the plug to make sure it is making proper contact. Sometimes, when there are two or three appliances all plugged into one cube connector in turn plugged into an outlet, the trouble can lie in a loose plug or cube. Next, slowly turn the cold control knob to maximum. If this doesn't turn the unit on, try pounding lightly against the temperature control. Sometimes this control sticks. If none of these efforts gets the unit going, there is nothing you can do but accept the condition, at least for the time being.

In the case of a refrigerator breakdown, eat the most perishable foods first. Let whatever ice cubes may be present in the ice trays be. They will help keep the food cold—you are running an icebox now. So do not use the refrigerator to cool things down the way you used to do. For example, do not place warm soda or beer in it. Doing so will warm up everything already inside a little and shorten its safe-cold period. With care, you can keep foods safely chilled for up to 24 hours this way.

If it is your freezer that has broken down, don't run off seeking to purchase dry ice. It isn't necessary. If you keep the freezer door closed as much as possible and do not place anything warm inside, the food now frozen will remain frozen for about two days.

Too cold. First make certain the control is turned to the proper minimum temperature setting. Then inspect the temperature sensing device. It is usually a thin metal tube terminating in a small metal bulb. See that the bulb is not covered with ice, frost, or paper, any of which can insulate it and so make it operate improperly. If this is not the trouble, shut the machine off for a few hours at a time.

Noise. One sign of a refrigeration unit's age is its increased noise. It makes the same noise it always has, but louder. When the noise is not only louder but different look for a broken spring support that is permitting the compressor to strike the case. Remove the pieces of spring and force a thick piece of rubber into the space the spring occupied. Also look for something metallic that has worked its way between the compressor and the machine's case. This could be a spoon or knife that has slipped inside. If so, remove it.

FROZEN NUTS, BOLTS, AND SCREWS

Nuts and bolts. Try a few drops of Liquid Wrench or a similar loosening solvent. Tap the nut or bolt while applying the solvent. The vibration often helps the solvent penetrate. If you have no solvent, try a little kerosene, charcoal-fire starting fluid, thin oil, or oil mixed with a little gasoline.

Heat the nut with a propane torch to expand it and then apply ice to the bolt to shrink it. Try removing the nut while it is still hot. This may not work the first time, but repeated application of heat, with or without cold, to the bolt will usually loosen the nut. Sometimes a drop of oil on the threads after the nut has been heated helps. If you do not have heat, try the ice alone—dry ice if you can get it. (Ice-cream trucks usually carry dry ice.)

An alternative to heating the nut while you cool the bolt consists of increasing the leverage on your wrench. You can do this by slipping the wrench handle into a piece of pipe. Sometimes you can do it by placing a second wrench on the handle of the first; this is awkward, but it can increase your leverage tremendously.

Fairly large nuts or bolt heads can sometimes be loosened by hammering. The point of a center punch or chisel is placed against one edge of the nut and driven into the nut in a direction tangent to the nut's perimeter with a hammer. This technique is not much help on a small nut or bolt head, but tremendous rotary force can be developed this way when the nut is more than an inch wide.

Screws. The problem here is that it is often impossible to get the point of the screwdriver to remain in the slot. As torque is increased the screwdriver jumps out of the slot. Sometimes you can arrange a lever to hold the driver in place and use a wrench on the driver's shaft to get the leverage you need. When this cannot be done, use the center punch technique previously described.

Sheared screw slot. Use the center punch technique, if you can. An alternate technique consists of drilling a hole into the screw for an inch or more and removing the screw (or bolt with a stripped head) with a screw extractor. If you have no extractor on hand, drive the tang end of a file into the hole and use that to rotate the screw and so remove it.

Screws in wood. Sometimes you can loosen a recalcitrant wood screw by holding the tip of a soldering iron to its head long enough to make it hot. This dries the adjoining wood a little and sometimes facilitates removal.

A few drops of Liquid Wrench on the threads of a frozen nut will do wonders to loosen it.

If the rust solvent will not loosen the nut, try heating it. Obviously a propane torch is best, but if you have no torch on hand, use your lighter.

Still another way to remove a recalcitrant nut is to increase your leverage. In this case, extending the handle of a lug wrench with a piece of pipe multiplies applied torque several times.

When a slot on a screw head has been so badly chewed up a screwdriver won't take hold, try turning the screw with the aid of a center punch and hammer.

When you can't secure sufficient leverage to turn a bolt or screw with a screwdriver alone, use a wrench on its shaft. Shaft is round? Use a small stillson wrench.

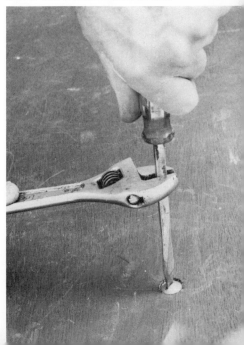

GARBAGE DISPOSER

Won't start. Push the reset button on the side of the motor. If the unit still won't operate, check the fuses or circuit breaker.

Hums but won't run. Shut the unit off and remove any knives, forks, or pieces of metal that may be inside. Turn the power on again. If the unit still will not run, take a stick (*never your hand*) and use it to turn the grind-ring turntable. This may free the ring and it will then spin, *so be careful.*

To prevent the ring from jamming and clogging make sure you use plenty of water when using the disposer, and do not force waste down into the disposer.

Vibrates. Tighten the bolts that hold the unit to the bottom of the sink. If that increases the vibration, something has badly damaged the grind-ring and/or its supporting motor shaft. Loosen the supporting bolts until you have time to determine and eliminate the cause of the vibration. But do not operate the disposer in this condition for more than a day or two. The vibration will loosen the supporting bolts to where they will permit the unit to drop or tilt seriously.

Sluggish. The cutters on the grind-ring may be worn or broken off. The drain-pipe of the disposer may be clogged. There is nothing you can do to improve the grind-ring, but you can improve the overall operation of the disposer by clearing the drainpipe. This is best done by disconnecting the pipe and poking it clean with a wire or snake. Do not use chemical drain openers; they can damage the motor.

GUTTERS AND LEADERS

Clogged gutter. Gutters filled with leaves and similar debris can be cleaned without climbing to the roof by making the tool shown in the illustration.

Sagging gutter. You can lift a gutter up temporarily by placing a long 2 x 4 beneath it or by driving a nail into the roof and lifting the gutter with wire. Pour water into the gutter after you have done this to check on the pitch.

Leaking gutter. Very small holes can be plugged directly with asphalt. Larger holes can be plugged by coating the hole and surrounding area with asphalt and then pressing a flat piece of metal over the hole. For larger holes the best patches are made by fitting short pieces of similar gutter material within the gutter. The patch can be held in place either with asphalt, as described, or by making holes through the patch and gutter and driving self-tapping metal screws into the holes. If you do not have a section of metal or plastic of suitable shape, bend an asphalt roofing tile to shape, or use some tar paper folded into the necessary channel shape.

Clogged leaders. Debris that has gathered at the lower end of a leader can be easily removed with the help of a piece of stiff wire, the end of which is bent into a small hook. When the blockage is at the top of a leader, you can often clear it using the tool suggested for cleaning a gutter.

Small holes in a gutter can be plugged with roof cement or tar.

Large holes in gutter require roof cement plus some kind of lining. In this case a section of identical gutter is used, but you can also use almost anything that can be bent to fit.

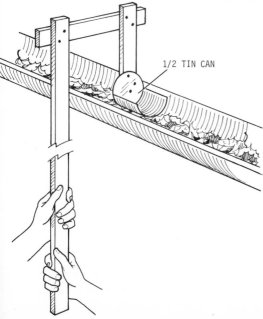

1/2 TIN CAN

When you have no means of reaching the gutter, you can still clear it with the aid of this tool.

HEATING: GAS FIRED HOT-AIR SYSTEM

No heat. Check the furnace thermostat to make certain it is properly positioned. Check the outdoor temperature if you have a dual-thermostat system. It is possible that the outdoor temperature is too high for the burner to go on although it is uncomfortably cool indoors.

If there is a strong smell of gas when you go to the cellar door to investigate further, remove yourself and your family as quickly as possible. Call the police from a neighbor's house. Let the experts take care of the problem.

If there is no gas smell see if the pilot light is on. If it is not, relight it following the instructions on the side of the furnace. If the pilot light is on and the burners are not, adjust the pilot flame so that it is a little larger. If that does not release the valve feeding the burners, the automatic control may be defective. Its repair or replacement is beyond the scope of this book.

Little heat. If the burners go on properly and there is little heat in any of the rooms, the trouble may be due to a dust-filled filter effectively blocking the flow of air. Remove and clean it. If that is not possible, operate without the filter until you can get a replacement.

Another possible cause is a defective fan motor. If the motor is not turning, press the little red button on its upper side, if there is one. This is a thermal safety switch; pushing it down recloses it. If the motor starts and keeps going, your problem is solved. If the motor starts and stops, something is overloading it. Shut off the furnace. Remove the furnace fuse for safety and then see if a little oil on the motor bearings or the fan bearings will not loosen it.

Another cause could be a broken fan belt. If the fan doesn't rotate little heat will reach the rooms. Any V-belt that will fit can be used. Take the old belt to a service station or an auto parts shop; they may have a useful replacement for you.

A less likely but not impossible cause could be that someone has closed the valves in the air ducts leading to the rooms. See that they are in the open position.

HEATING:

OIL FIRED HOT-WATER SYSTEMS

Burner doesn't fire. In the normal sequence of events, the burner doesn't always fire immediately when the thermostat calls for heat. (The demand setting is higher than the room temperature pointer.) Depending on the temperature of the water at the moment, the circulating pump may go on first and run for a few minutes before the burner is ignited. Therefore, do not jump to the conclusion your heating system is in trouble if you do not hear the mild whomp of the burner when you turn the thermostat.

If after 5 minutes the burner still has not fired, check to make certain no one has accidentally turned off the safety switch at the head of the cellar stairs, and

All properly wired heating systems have two manual shut-off switches. One at the entrance to the cellar or basement, the other on the side of the furnace. This one is on the side of an oil-burning furnace.

that the switch on the side of the furnace has not been turned off either. Next, check the furnace fuse by replacing it. If the furnace still doesn't start, check the other fuses in the box. They may be incorrectly labeled.

Next turn the thermostat all the way down and then all the way up. If this doesn't start the burner, remove the thermostat's cover. If it is of the type that has electrical contacts, blow them clean. If it has a small mercury switch, work the thermostat by turning it up and down. This will tilt the switch. If you can see a spark inside the switch, there is control power on the switch and this portion of the equipment is probably satisfactory. If you cannot see a small spark, the furnace may not be receiving electrical power or a wire leading to the thermostat may be broken, or the control circuit (transformer, etc.) may be defective.

Assuming you can see a spark and the contact points are clean, turn the thermostat to a high temperature, return to the furnace and listen to it. If it is silent, give a few light raps to the metal box fastened to the side of the chimney. The box carries a chimney thermostat which projects into the chimney and in time becomes soot-laden and corroded. Tapping the box often loosens the thermostat mechanism and sets it working again, at least for a while. If tapping doesn't help, push or slide the red button you will find on the side of the box. If the burner starts and keeps going, fine. If the burner starts and stops shortly afterwards, do not push the button a second time. This is as far as you can go in this direction without additional information, which is beyond the scope of this book.

On the other hand, if upon approaching the furnace you hear a high-pitched

Remove the thermostat's dust cover, blow the dust out, rotate the control from high to low, and check for a spark.

Control button on this chimney thermostat is above the mechanic's index finger.

Indoor oil tanks usually have a float-type oil level indicator such as this one.

sound—the sound of an electrical spark—the trouble is most likely a lack of oil in your tank. Although modern oil suppliers keep track of the weather and your needs, this does sometimes happen, so check your tank's oil level. Read the oil-level meter if you have one, or use a long stick or a stone tied to a rope to measure the oil level. If there are only a few inches of oil, your oil filters and possibly nozzle are most certainly clogged. But don't bother to do anything about it. The oil on the bottom of your tank is almost invariably muck. It will foul your filters almost as soon as you clean them.

However, if you have a foot or more of oil in your tank, there is a chance the overload switch on the motor has opened. If you can find a little red button on the top of your pump motor frame, push it. If the motor starts and keeps going, you are out of trouble. If the motor stops, something is keeping it from turning properly. This means dismantling the entire apparatus, which is again beyond the scope of this book.

If you can hear the motor turning as well as the sound of the ignition spark and there is oil in the tank, there is a good chance that cleaning the filter(s) and the nozzle will be all that is needed to return the furnace to operation.

Open the furnace safety switch at the head of the stairs and also the switch at the side of the furnace. Now you can open and clean the filter(s) and the nozzle. Unfortunately, since there are dozens of different burner designs in use, there is no single set of instructions that will lead you to the filter(s). However, if you

The finger points to the overload switch reset button. Press it once. If the burner starts up and keeps going, fine. If it starts and stops a few minutes later, do not press the button again. Something is overloading the motor and continued operation can cause damage.

unscrew every large nut you find on the pump and remove every large cover, you will reach the filter. You can do no harm doing any of this as long as you take care not to damage the gaskets and do not tamper with any screws.

To get to the nozzle you have to remove the burner. Close the oil line valves and disconnect them. Then unbolt the burner and move it backwards carefully out of the furnace. Generally there is sufficient play in the electrical cable to permit you to do this without disconnecting it. Unscrew the nozzle, which is at the tip of the burner. Clean its hole out with a pin. Then remove and clean the filter you may find directly behind the nozzle. Try not to disturb the points (long porcelain insulators terminating in metal tips) when you do this. Reassemble and try again.

If you do not hear a spark when approaching the furnace, but do smell oil, run back out of the furnace room, up the stairs and open the safety switch you will find there. What is happening is that the pump is filling the interior of the furnace with fine drops of oil, as it should, but there is no ignition—no spark. This is a dangerous condition as a spark at this time can cause an explosion.

There is a possibility that lack of spark is caused by one of the high-tension wires (it looks like an auto ignition wire) having separated from the points. (The ignition wires snap on.) There is also a small chance that the points have swung together, touching each other, or that the gap between them, which should be about ⅛ inch across, has been closed with soot. Any of these conditions can prevent ignition, but the chance of their occurrence is very small, and to check you generally have to remove the burner from the furnace.

Burner operates but there is little heat. This may be caused by lack of water in the system, in which case you will have heat in the lower-floor radiators and little or no heat in the upper-floor radiators. The trouble may be due to a water-feed valve that has been closed by mistake or an improperly adjusted automatic-feed valve. To increase the flow of water into the boiler, loosen the lock nut on top of the valve and turn the screw into the valve.

If you find some of the radiators on one floor are hot while others are cold (although their valves are open), the cause could be a closed zone-control valve. Examine the large pipes coming out of the furnace. See that no valve leading to a portion of your home is closed. This would be a zone valve.

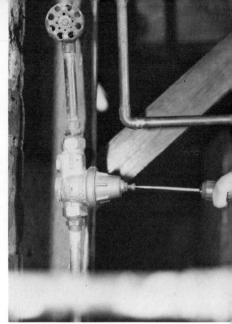

The altitude pointer on this triple gauge indicates the height in feet of the water in the heating system. When the pointer drops below its normal position, your top-floor radiators are not filled with water, as they should be, and are therefore cold.

To increase the pressure of the water in your hot-water heating system and thus fill all the radiators, loosen the lock nut and turn in the control screw on the feed valve.

If a radiator is only partially hot although its valve is open, the trouble is due to air in the radiator; you must bleed it. Simply open the little setscrew you will find in the center of the small tube projecting from the radiator. If you do not have the key (a small wrench), use a pair of long-nosed pliers. If you have neither, unscrew the metal projection after you have closed the valve and prepared yourself for a possible flood by placing a bucket underneath. Then open the valve a fraction and let the water slowly into the radiator. Close the radiator valve when water emerges from the hole and replace the projection.

HEATING: OIL-FIRED STEAM SYSTEM

Burner doesn't fire. Everything that has been suggested for curing oil-fired hot-water system burners applies equally to oil-fired steam systems. In addition, there may be a pressure-sensitive switch and a low-water cutoff switch. The pressure-sensitive switch shuts the burner off if steam pressure goes too high. Unless the switch is defective it would not prevent the burner from going on. The low-water safety switch is there to prevent firing should the boiler water level go too low. If this is the case, use the manual controls to let more water into the boiler.

Individual radiator cold. This may be due to a closed radiator feed valve. In the better installations these valves are usually gate valves, which means a half dozen turns or more are required to fully open or close them. Check that your valve is turned all the way. Lack of heat or slow heating may also be caused by a defective air-release valve. To check, shut the radiator off. Remove the air-release valve by unscrewing it. Open the feed valve. If everything else is working properly you will hear the sound of air leaving the radiator and soon see steam. Shut the feed valve at this point. You cannot safely operate a radiator without the air-release valve. Replace the valve if you can or try cleaning it out by placing it in boiling water to which a little washing soda has been added.

Noise. Noise at the radiator itself can be caused by the radiator being tilted the wrong way. The end away from the feed pipe should be higher by an inch or so than the feed pipe end. Use blocks of wood as necessary. Another possible cause is a partially open feed valve having a loose stem. Open the valve all the way, or close it all the way.

Noise in the pipes can be caused by one or more pipes having moved so that they touch something, causing squeaks as the pipes move with temperature changes. If the pipes have sagged, water collects in the low portion of the pipes and is buffeted by the passage of the steam. Using wire lift the pipes back into their proper positions.

HEATING PROBLEMS:
GENERAL RECOMMENDATIONS

Insufficient heat. You can direct more heat to one particular room or a few rooms by diverting heat from other rooms. Simply partially close the radiators and registers in the rooms that require less heat. Do not close them completely in very cold weather as that may lead to freezing.

An alternative is to place a fan behind or even in front of the radiator from which you desire more heat. The movement of the air over the radiator will extract considerably more heat than the radiator would otherwise normally supply.

Emergency heat. Assuming your normal central-heating system is not functioning and cannot be repaired at this time, you can heat a small portion of your home by burning a fire in the fireplace. If you run out of wood, roll newspaper up in tight bundles and burn it like wood. You can also burn coal or coke in a fireplace if you start with a wood fire.

See COOKING IN EMERGENCIES for additional fire-making and stove suggestions. Bear in mind that none of these measures can possibly heat your home the way your central-heating system normally does. But they can keep you and your family alive and reasonably well. Therefore, do not try to heat more than a small space. Gather round the source of heat, whatever it may be. Close off all the other rooms, and if the temperature has dropped, protect your pipes against freezing by draining them. And don't forget, *no matter how cold it may get, you must have a little air in the room.*

Keeping warm. If the heat is off in your home, put on additional clothes, which should not be tight, before you begin to feel cold. Remember, if you let yourself get thoroughly chilled waiting for the heat to be repaired, you will have great difficulty getting warm again and there will be a good chance you will become ill. Don't be too proud to sit around in an overcoat, gloves, hat, and overshoes. Should you become so chilled you cannot stop shivering, get into a hot tub of water, when the hot water is restored. Drink hot liquids but not alcoholic beverages. Remember, the temperature does not have to be very low to become dangerously chilled.

If you have turned the heat down in your bedroom to conserve heat or if the heat is off, place two or more blankets *beneath* the bottom sheet. You need two blankets under you for every blanket on top to keep comfortable. If the temperature is really down, sleep in your clothing. Wear a soft hat and warm socks. That's the way our forefathers did it before steam heat.

HOT WATER: GAS-FIRED BOILER

Correcting the water temperature. If the water is cool, inspect the tank. The pilot light may be out. Relight following the instructions on the side of the tank. If the main burners do not go on, try making the pilot light a little larger. If the burner is going strong, check the temperature setting. Check the valves to make certain the cold water is not bypassing the tank.

If the water starts hot but turns cold quickly, the tank is old and lined with lime. Its capacity has been reduced. There is nothing to be done except turn the thermostat up a little.

If the water is too hot, the thermostat is turned too high; turn it back.

You will find the drain valve for a modern gas-fired boiler beneath the control cover. Before draining the tank, be certain to open a hot-water faucet upstairs, to let the air into the tank as it drains. Note the instructions for relighting the pilot on the side of the tank.

Tank leaks. If the leak is small and you need hot water immediately, let it leak. If you can do without hot water, shut the unit off and drain it, after first opening a hot-water faucet upstairs somewhere to let air into the tank. If the tank is of galvanized iron and the hole is small, you can possibly plug the hole with Plumber Seal, which is a trade name for hand-moldable epoxy. Just mix the two sticks thoroughly together and force some of the epoxy putty into the hole so that it locks itself in place. A large hole can be plugged with a large self-tapping metal screw, a washer, and a small piece of sheet rubber. You can purchase this screw plug in a hardware supply shop. As an alternative, when the hole is large enough you can use a Molly bolt or a toggle bolt. In any case, be advised that unless the hole was made by a rifle bullet, the tank is more than ready for replacement.

If the tank is of copper and insulated you will have to cut a hole in the outer metal shell and push the insulation aside to get to the tank itself. Since the copper of the tank is not very thick to begin with, it is probably quite thin around the hole, which means that you cannot use a bolt of any kind to plug the hole. The best approach is to rub the surface of the copper bright with steel wool for a distance of 2 or more inches each side of the hole. Then bend a piece of copper sheet to fit the curve of the tank and sweat (solder) it in place. You will need a propane torch for this. No iron will be large enough.

As an alternative you can cement the copper patch in place with epoxy. It will hold if you roughen the mating surfaces with steel wool, make the patch large enough and the water pressure isn't too high.

If the inner tank is of glass, there is nothing that can be done to remedy a leak.

HOT-WATER HEATING FURNACE

If the water is only lukewarm although the furnace is operating normally, someone has mistakenly turned the mixing valve all the way in the wrong direction. Turn the valve the other way.

If the water is too hot, turn the mixing valve in the other direction a fraction of a turn or adjust the hydrostat on the furnace to a lower temperature.

Varying the position of the mixer-valve control will vary the percentage of hot water mixed with cold that enters the hot-water pipes leading to your faucets and equipment.

If the water starts hot but soon turns lukewarm, this is due to aging (liming) of the water-heating coils. Reducing the rate of flow of the hot water out of the faucet will usually increase the temperature of the water. You can also turn the hydrostat up a little, but never beyond 200° F, and you can also adjust the mixing valve to permit more hot water to flow and less cold. Both these moves can be dangerous, as the water coming out of the hot-water tap may be near boiling when the tap is first opened.

HOT WATER: STEAM-HEATED

If the water starts hot but soon turns lukewarm, this is due to aging (liming) of the water-heating coils. As previously suggested, draw the hot water at a lower rate from the tap. This will give the water more time in the heating coils, and it will therefore come out hotter from the tap. As previously suggested, you can also turn up the hydrostat on the furnace and reduce the quantity of cold water the mixing valve adds to the hot water.

Another common cause of hot-water trouble is lack of water in the steam boiler. If the water level is below its normal height, the production of hot water will be reduced. Some home owners operate their steam boilers with a little more water than suggested by the manufacturer to make certain this doesn't happen.

HOT WATER: ELECTRICALLY HEATED

If the water is cold, look for a blown fuse and check that the thermostat is not in the off position.

If the water is lukewarm, the thermostat is probably incorrectly set. Adjust it correctly.

If the water starts hot then quickly cools, the tank has aged. There is nothing to be done except turn the thermostat up a little and give the tank time enough to heat up completely before drawing a large quantity of hot water.

INTRUDERS

Each year millions of homes are burglarized, billions of dollars in goods are stolen and destroyed, and each year thousands are mugged, raped, assaulted, and even killed within their own homes. The instructions that follow will not solve the terrible problem, but they can greatly reduce the chance that your home will be robbed and that you and your loved ones will be harmed.

Criminals that enter the home can be divided into two groups: those who hate society and are seeking any excuse and any means for violating persons and property, and those who desire nothing more than gain. Fortunately, the mere gain seekers—the burglars—outnumber the muggers, rapists, and killers six to one. The chance that an intruder will do you bodily harm is therefore only one in six.

Another fact to be noted is that most rapists, assaulters, and child molesters are known to the victim. This may seem to confuse the situation, but doesn't really. Play it this way. If you have never seen the intruder before, you can be fairly certain his only intent is robbery. If the individual is someone whom you have seen before and who should be elsewhere in the ordinary course of events; if his or her presence gives you an uneasy feeling (and in these matters it is always wise to trust your feelings), you may well be facing assault and/or rape.

A third point to remember is that robbers usually return to the scene of their crime if they have been successful. If there has been a robbery in your area and the thieves have not been caught, there is a good chance there will be another robbery in a short time. Their reasoning is logical; the heist was easy, the haul was worth their time, why not return. Some apartment-house dwellers have been robbed half a dozen times while living in the same apartment.

Prevention. Don't make entry easy. Make certain all your locks are secure and that all first-floor and basement windows are securely latched. Don't hide keys under the doormat, in the mail box, or on top of the door frame. Don't leave the garage door unlocked.

Get a dog, preferably the loud-barking kind. (This writer lives in an area known as Dog Patch; there is at least one dog in every home. There has been no robbery here in 15 years.) A burglar is not afraid of house dogs, but he doesn't want attention drawn to himself. In a doggy neighborhood, when one dog barks they all bark. Then backyard floodlights are switched on and people look out their windows and report intruders.

You can of course purchase a trained watch/attack dog, and they are completely safe if you warn your friends that they cannot drop casually by. A large attack dog is a wonderful protection for someone living alone. Not only are they pleasant companions, but they turn into fanged missiles upon command. Even a gentle house dog will attack if you are assaulted and scream for help.

Install electronic protection. The range and variety of equipment available, much of which you can install yourself, are beyond the scope of this book. But you should know that there is equipment that can detect footfalls any distance from your home; that can detect the most careful burglar and render him helpless with high-powered sound; that can warn police silently; that does not fail even if the local power system quits and that will even report a fire to the fire department automatically.

Do not admit anyone to your home without proper identification, and if you somehow sense the identification is false, check it out by telephoning the supposed company.

Wrong-number calls should be politely turned away. There is no need to give your number to anyone who has called your home by mistake.

Beware the emergency phone calls that purport to require your immediate presence. Should you receive a call informing you that your child or your father has been hurt and is in the local hospital calling for you, phone the hospital before rushing down there. If they are indeed in a hospital, someone is taking care of them. The minute or two necessary to make certain no criminal is drawing you out of your home so that he can rob you may save you a lot of money. If you find the alarm is false, phone the police and follow their instructions.

Don't advertise your absence. Don't report your forthcoming world tour to the local press. Don't leave your home unattended. Hire a house sitter or at least arrange for someone to come in every day, turn lights on and off, cut the grass, open and close the garage door occasionally to make the home look lived in. If you have pets, have the caretaker walk them. It is easy enough to get a highschool kid to do this for a small fee. Usually, this will cost you less than leaving the animals at the vet. And inform the police of your plans. They will keep an extra careful watch on your home.

It is common for crooks planning to burgle a particular home to scout the area to see how the roads run, the path the police car takes, how often it passes, what the general habits of the householders are. Should you or your neighbors see any individual on foot or in a car pass up and down your streets a few times without good reason, inform the police. Also report all suspicious moving vans and trucks. No one moves without informing their neighbors. If there is a moving truck backed up to a home in your neighborhood and no sign of the owner, phone the police.

Confrontations. If on coming home you encounter someone on your doorstep whom you haven't invited, whom you may have seen staring at you at the supermarket or elsewhere, don't be polite. Don't invite them in. If they manage to push past you or talk you out of stopping them and get inside, or if you find them inside your home with a flimsy excuse such as that the door was open, run outside if there are other people nearby, or if you can, run into a neighbor's home. If you can't do that, smile, make an excuse. Go to the phone and quietly call the police.

Do not threaten. To make a threat is merely to warn the intruder of your suspicion. Put them off with an offer of a drink or anything else that comes to mind and calmly call for help. Remember, many people get trapped by criminals because they hesitate to be impolite, to chance insulting an innocent individual by calling in the police, or to risk being mistaken and appearing foolish. No intelligent individual will misunderstand your fear and precautions. The police would much rather come to your home and receive an apology for a false call than come to your home to pick up a corpse.

Burglar in the house. If upon coming home you believe there is a burglar present, just leave and call for help from a neighbor. (This is where any kind of watchdog is worth his dog biscuit. You'd know someone was there.) If you are in one part of the house and hear a burglar coming in through the front door or window, just leave if you can without being noticed. If you are upstairs and they are downstairs, don't take a chance on meeting them. Stay quietly put and phone the police.

If you believe there is a prowler outside your home, call the police if your area is patrolled. If you live outside a patrolled area, turn the lights on, wake everyone up. Stay away from the windows; that makes you an easy target. To check if the prowler is still there, turn the lights off before you peek out.

If you inadvertently walk in on a burglar rifling your home, don't scream, don't panic, don't threaten. Just stand quietly to one side, out of his path to the door.

Do not stare and give the impression you are memorizing their physical characteristics. But if you can observe without being obvious about it, *do memorize* such characteristics as features, height, and color of hair and eyes.

If the burglar asks to be directed to your valuables, direct him. Do not remonstrate. Do not argue. Play the part of a good loser. He has outsmarted you. This satisfaction is a major portion of his goal. Should you take it upon yourself to criticize his morals, should you warn him in the classic fashion, "You'll never get away with this," you will rob him of part of the satisfaction he gets from stealing. You will make him feel bad and very likely he will lay into you to make himself feel like a winner again. So do what you are told to do and stay alive.

Dealing with a rapist. Police are of two minds when advising women of the action they should take when faced with a rapist. Some say fight, some say don't fight. Actually, the choice is clear enough. If you think you can win, fight. If you do not believe you can win, don't. No one gets as badly beaten as a half-hearted fighter. Make up your mind quickly and *attack* before you are in serious danger; before you are cornered; before you are on the ground and helpless.

Smile, toss something towards his face—a balled-up handkerchief, a cigarette, anything at all to catch his eye. Then kick for the groin and keep on kicking. Remember, one good kick and this man will never think rape again. If this appears to be brutal, bear in mind the fact that a rapist is not a poor, sex-starved unfortunate. He is not driven by lust, but by hate. He hates the world. He wants revenge. Rape is his way of killing you. (Many of them do kill after it is over.) If you can't get a good kick in, find a weapon—any weapon, a bottle, knife, fork, fireplace poker. If you are in his arms, go for the jugular with your teeth. Your rapist has a terrible, consuming hatred of you. Go soft after you have started to fight and you are finished. And while you are fighting, make as much noise as you can. Throw things through the windows and scream like you have never screamed before.

IRON, ELECTRIC

Won't heat. Look for a bad connection between the plug and the iron. Try moving the temperature control switch to a higher temperature setting; that may get it working (without thermostatic control). Hold the iron to the desired temperature by unplugging and plugging it and again as it gets too hot and too cold.

No steam. Make certain there is water in the iron. Make sure you have waited long enough for the iron to produce steam by using the old tailor's trick of putting a wet finger to the bottom of the iron. If there is a hiss when you apply your finger lightly, steam should be issuing from the iron. If there is no steam, pull the plug immediately out of the wall. Under no circumstances let the iron remain on. *It will explode.* Wait until the disconnected iron is cold, then use a thin, stiff wire to poke the steam vent holes open. This done, try the iron cautiously again.

Iron sticks. Let the iron warm. Carefully scrape the bottom of the iron clean with a butter knife and wash it with soap and water. If necessary, use a scouring pad to remove all traces of the gum that has collected, but take care not to scratch the pressing surface.

LIGHTNING

Warning signals. Lightning storms are usually presaged by a small but sudden dip in temperature and barometric pressure, a gathering of low-flying cumulus clouds, and sometimes, when a bolt is imminent and certain to be close, you can feel your skin tingle.

The approach of a lightning storm can be roughly measured by timing the intervals between the flash and the boom. Count the intervening seconds and then divide the number by four. Since light on earth is, for all practical purposes, instantaneous, and sound requires four seconds to traverse a mile, every four seconds you count off between the flash and the boom indicates a space of a mile between yourself and the lightning. As the storm comes closer the time intervals shorten. The booms no longer roll ponderously across the sky, but become sharper and sharper until the flash and the sound occur simultaneously, and the sound is a sharp, ripping crack. Closer still and you can smell the brimstone (ozone). Generally, but not always, when it begins to rain the danger of lightning is gone.

Protection. If you live high on a windy hill, as the song goes, you are well advised to hire an expert to install a lightning rod on your home. It is not that you cannot do this yourself, it is not that difficult. But if the rod is not installed properly, if there aren't a sufficient number of heavy conductors running from the rod to a good ground, the rod is worse than useless. *It will attract lightning to your home.*

If you have a TV antenna up on your roof, you should safeguard your home and TV receiver with a lightning arrester. This is a low-cost, easily connected device that only requires a heavy copper wire running to a pipe driven into moist earth to be highly effective. Connected this way, TV antennas offer a small degree of lightning protection.

If you are planning to re-side your home, choose aluminum siding. Even if the siding is not grounded, it will provide a degree of protection against lightning. This is not provided by plastic siding.

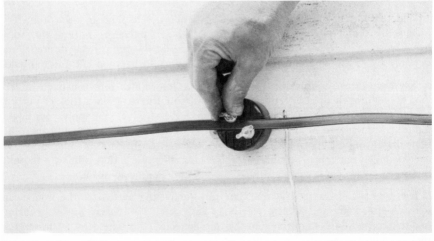

When installing a TV antenna lightning arrester, use 14-gauge or heavier wire for grounding.

During a storm. If you are indoors, stay away from windows and doors. Stay away from pipes and electrical wires that run up through or near the roof, as for example water pipes. Do not take a bath or shower until the storm has passed and moved on a goodly distance. Do not bother to turn your TV receiver or radio off. Lightning can strike your antenna regardless of whether or not the set is turned on. By the same token do not go near the set during the storm.

If you are in an automobile, pull off the road, taking care not to park under a tree. Remain in the car until the storm is over. Being of metal, the car will protect you.

If you are out in an open field and the storm is still a few miles away, go to the nearest large building. Do not take shelter in a tent or small shack. If the storm is close, lie down on the earth. Never mind the muck and wet. It is better to be wet than dead. And never run for shelter beneath a single tree or a small group of trees. That is asking for a flashy departure from this world. However, if you are close to a dense forest, enter the forest. Some of the trees may be struck by lightning, but the chance of lightning striking the tree you have chosen isn't too great.

If you are on the beach, run for shelter in a large building if there is time. If there is no time, lie flat on the sand. Never enter the water. If you are in the water and the storm is a distance off, run out. If the storm is close, remain fully immersed. The worse thing you can do is stand up in shallow water. That makes you the best target on the beach.

If you are in a boat and have time, come into shore and run for shelter. If there is no shelter, get off the dock and lie flat on the nearby soil. If the storm is close to your boat, lie flat in the lowest portion of the boat.

If someone near is struck by lightning, you can go to their aid. Lightning doesn't remain in the struck individual. It is safe to touch him or her. About half the people hit by lightning survive. Start artificial respiration immediately and send for medical help.

LOCKS

Broken key. If you have another key, use a pair of tweezers or even a safety pin to pry the piece of key out of the lock. If you do not have another key and the key is broken near its bow or handle, push the key in the rest of the way. Then poke the end of a screwdriver or the tip of a nail file into the space between the key and the lock and try to rotate the key as you normally would.

Locked out, exterior doors. An expert with the proper tools can pick most locks (but not all locks) in a few minutes. If you are not similarly prepared, put off your lock picking until you have tried all other means of gaining entry.

If you are like many other home owners, you may possibly have forgotten to lock all the doors and windows. It pays to look and see.

If there is a double-hung window you can reach, use a butter knife or similar flat piece of metal to release the window latch as shown on next page.

If there is no other way and you must get into your home quickly, break a window. To do this without risking injury, cover your hand and wrist with a glove or a cloth and gently tap a large stone against the glass until it cracks.

If your key breaks off inside the lock, try turning the remains of the key with the help of a nail file or small screwdriver.

Using a thin knife to open a window latch.

A dead bolt can be released following the method to be described provided that there is a small space between the door and its frame, or you can make one by removing the trim, and that the bolt can be moved backwards. On some locks this is impossible. You also need at least one ice pick, preferably two.

Place the point of one pick firmly against the bolt and swing the pick handle so that the bolt is moved back towards the lock a fraction of an inch. If you have a second pick, use it to hold the bolt in place while you remove and reposition the first ice pick. Next, you use the pick again as a lever to force the bolt back a little more. This is repeated until the bolt is all the way back in its lock and the door is freed. Without the second pick to help you hold the bolt in position, you must either press firmly against the door or pull it towards yourself. The purpose of either of these two moves is to hold the bolt in place by friction.

A latch bolt differs from a dead bolt in that the end of the bolt—the one that enters the hole in the strike plate—is beveled.

To move a latch bolt back and out of the hole in the strike plate you need a strip of plastic such as a credit card or a butter knife or a similar strip of flexible, flat metal. You also need a little space between the door and its frame. If there isn't any, remove the interfering door trim. Push the edge of the credit card or metal strip between the door and its frame and against the beveled edge of the latch bolt. The pressure on the angled surface will force the latch bolt back.

When the door itself is unlocked and you are prevented from entering by a safety chain, there are two methods you can try to release the chain.

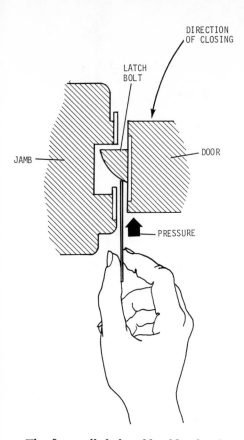

DIRECTION
OF CLOSING

LATCH
BOLT

JAMB

DOOR

PRESSURE

A credit card or similarly thin and flexible strip of plastic or metal can be used to open a latch bolt.

The first, called the old rubber-band trick, depends on the chain being long enough to enable you to slide your arm inside. If you can do this, attach a strip of masking or adhesive tape to a rubber band. Press the tape firmly against the inside of the door a foot or so away from the knob on the end of the safety chain. Stretch the rubber band and hook it over the knob on the chain. Close the door and the rubber band will release the chain for you.

How to use Scotch tape and a rubber band to detach a safety chain when you're locked out.

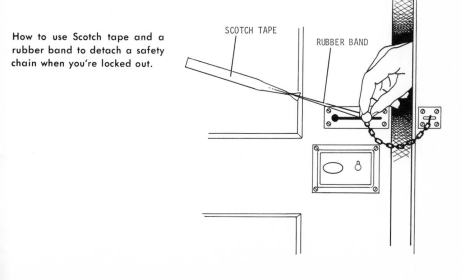

SCOTCH TAPE

RUBBER BAND

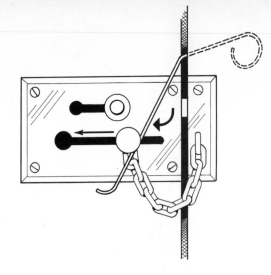

When you cannot get your hand
between the door and the frame
to use the rubber-band trick,
bend a wire as shown and use it
to detach the safety chain.

The other method can be tried when you can do no more than open the door a crack. The method consists of bending a length of wire into a hook, as shown, and turning the wire so that its hooked end engages and then unlocks the knob on the end of the chain.

Picking a lock. Lock picking should be reserved as your next-to-last-ditch effort to gain entry. Lock picking is not something one can master in one easy try. Still, this is an emergency, and there is nothing else to do but try.

Warded locks are the cast-iron locks that are operated by long iron keys erroneously called skeleton keys. They are the simplest of all locks and not difficult to pick.

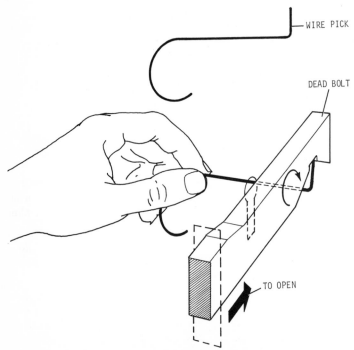

WIRE PICK

DEAD BOLT

TO OPEN

How to pick a warded lock.

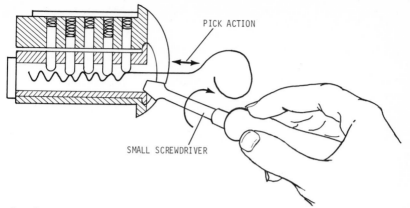

PICK ACTION

SMALL SCREWDRIVER

Despite what you see in the movies, it takes two hands to pick a pin tumbler. One hand is used to apply a continuous rotary pressure to the plug, the other hand (not shown) is used to saw the pick back and forth.

First, if you have any other skeleton keys on hand, try them all. One may work. Then make a pick by bending a ⅛-inch right angle on the end of a stiff piece of wire and then bending a loop in the same wire about 4 inches away from the right-angle bend. Insert the wire, short bend first, just as you would a key. Turn the wire, seeking to locate the slot in the dead bolt, and withdraw the bolt from the strike plate. The accompanying drawing illustrates the desired action.

A pin-tumbler lock is the type of lock used on almost every front door on every home in this country, so there is no problem about identifying it. (It is not used in automobiles.) Contrary to what you may have seen in the movies or on TV, two hands are necessary to pick it, one to turn the plug, the other to lift the pins out of the way.

Use a slim screwdriver or the point of a nail file to turn the plug. To do this place the point of the tool partway into the key slot and exert a light, constant rotary pressure on the plug in either direction. To lift the pins, bend a length of stiff wire into the shape shown in the drawing.

This is the action: While you maintain a rotary pressure with one hand on the plug, you insert the pick into the key slot, and saw the tool in and out of the slot as you exert a light upward pressure on it. Hopefully, there will be an instant when the laws of chance will operate in your favor and all the pins and drivers will be aligned properly. At this instant the plug will be released and you will turn it, opening the lock. In theory, this approach always works because sooner or later the pins and drivers must fall into the correct position. With beginners, it is almost always much later.

Forcing a lock. This is truly a last-ditch operation as you can very easily not only damage the lock beyond repair, you can also make it impossible to open the door without taking the lock apart from the inside.

If you have a drill, electric or manual, with a ¹⁄₁₆- to ³⁄₃₂-inch bit, drill a hole right into the lock, directly above the tumbler pins. (See illustration.) Now try turning the plug using a screwdriver as a key. If this is no go, bend a ¼-inch turn on the end of a stiff wire and use it to lift the drivers up and out of the way. If you are still unsuccessful, drive a large screwdriver into the key slot. Put a wrench to the screwdriver and see if you can force the plug to turn.

Drilling a lock free (left). The aim here is to drill through all the pins and pin drivers. Since this lock is upside down (as compared to the usual lock), the drill point is below the key slot. The interior view of a pin tumbler lock is shown below. Note the pins and pin drivers locking the plug and the position of the drill prior to drilling the plug (the part that rotates) free.

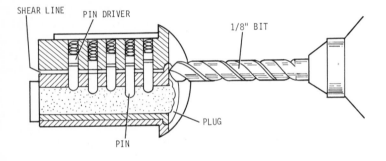

SHEAR LINE   PIN DRIVER   1/8" BIT

PLUG

PIN

An alternate method of forcing a lock which you can use before or after trying to drill the plug free consists of using a large Stillson wrench to unscrew the lock cylinder from the door. Inspect the rim of the lock cylinder. If there is a loose, protective flange behind its rim, drive a screwdriver beneath it and rip it off. Position the wrench on the rim of the lock cylinder and force the cylinder to turn counterclockwise. This will break the set screws holding the cylinder immobile and you will be able to unscrew the cylinder from the door, which will enable you to open the door.

If the lock is inside the doorknob, use a hacksaw to cut and separate the knob from the rest of the shaft. Then push the remaining lock parts inside the building and withdraw the bolt with a screwdriver. You can also use the Stillson wrench to rip the knob from its support and thus free the bolt.

Remember, any of these three methods can leave you with a wrecked lock and no farther inside than before. They are last-ditch methods.

Locked out, interior doors. If you have a locked closet door, try releasing the latch bolt as previously described. If the door is held by a warded lock, try picking it. If that doesn't work, and the hinge pins are on the outside, as they often are, remove them, slip a screwdriver between the door and its frame and pry the door free.

If you are desperate, try ripping the lock off with a large stillson wrench. This method can only be used with locks located within the door knob.

If you find yourself locked inside a closet, don't just scream. Your voice will not carry far. You will soon become hoarse and screaming may lead to panic. Instead, find a hard object such as a shoe or an umbrella. Bang a little, holler a little and wait. A steady noise does not attract as much attention as an intermittent noise.

These efforts failing, try sitting on the floor with your back to the wall and your feet flat against the bottom of the door. You can develop a very powerful push this way, sufficient, in many instances, to take a door right off its hinges. Should the wall be too far away to do this, place something behind your back. In situations where the closet—or room—is too large to do this, find a heavy object that you can swing against the door. A standard typewriter, for example, or a bowling ball would be just fine. Swing it against the lock side of the door, of course.

Bathroom doors are usually fitted with privacy locks. They have no key. The lock is operated from inside the room and is designed to merely provide privacy for the occupant.

Sometimes the lock will be accidentally closed with the door in the open position. When the door is closed from the outside, its lock closes and there is no one inside to open it. Sometimes a child will lock himself inside and be unable to open it. And sometimes someone will become ill and be unable to operate the lock. When any of these things occur, here are the steps you can take to open the bathroom door from the outside.

Inspect the doorknob. If there is a small hole in its center, poke a wire down the hole. That will release the latch. If the hole is about ¼ inch in diameter, slide a thin screwdriver into the hole. Find the slot, insert the driver and turn. That will release the latch. If there is no hole, utilize one of the following methods.

If there is a hole in the knob of a locked bathroom door, insert a small screwdriver and turn the slot the driver engages. If the hole is too small for a screwdriver, insert a stiff wire to release the lock.

Force the latch bolt back using a piece of plastic or a flat strip of metal as previously described.

Remove the trim from the doorframe near the doorknob. Position an automobile jack horizontally across the doorframe in line with the doorknob. Expand the jack and force the doorframe sufficiently apart to free the lock.

If there is no time, take a hammer or an ax and bash a hole in the door. If the door is perfectly smooth, choose a spot about 8 inches above and to the inside of the doorknob. The wood is very thin there. With a panel door, attack one of the panels. It is thin.

If you do not have a hammer or an ax and there is a wall close to and parallel to the bathroom door, sit on the floor. Place your back against the wall and push against the door with both feet. If there are two of you, both sit and push.

Should the locked door face an open room, do not charge the door with your shoulder unless you are wearing football shoulder pads and weigh 300 pounds. Instead, find a large piece of furniture—a bureau or breakfront. Line it up with the door and run it into the door just as hard as you can. If one ramming doesn't do it, back the furniture a dozen feet away from the door and charge again.

For opening an auto door see AUTOMOBILE: Locked out. (Note. Autos do not use pin-tumbler locks and cannot be picked as described.)

OVEN, ELECTRIC

Won't heat. This is most often caused by a burned out element. Usually, you can actually see the break in the heating rod. When this happens there is no alternative to replacing the element. When the oven switch is at fault, you can sometimes operate the oven by turning the switch to the time-bake position.

Note, when you clean the oven be very careful not to spill the oven-cleaning solution on the heating elements. The cleaning solutions presently sold are very strong alkalis and will eat through the iron and cause the element to burn out in a short time.

Thermostat inaccurate. Don't waste your time trying to correct an inaccurate thermostat. They are never perfect to begin with. Use an oven thermometer to find out how much the control is off and in what direction. Then simply adjust the control setting as necessary. If the thermostat is completely haywire and won't turn the oven down, turn the oven on and off manually until you have time to replace the thermostat.

OVEN, GAS

A gas oven is a gas range enclosed in a box. Everything suggested in regard to gas ranges is applicable to gas ovens. The only difference is the thermostat. If it is accurate or near accurate, let it be. If it is highly inaccurate, either compensate by adjusting the setting or the control or wait until you have the time to replace the entire unit.

PIPES, LEAKING

First, close the main valve. You will find it next to the water meter. Next, open a hot and cold water faucet in any portion of the house that is lower than the burst pipe. Then go to a floor above the hole in the pipe and open another hot and cold water faucet. All this is done to drain the water out of the broken pipe before the water flows onto the floor, and to prevent more water from entering the pipe.

Use one of the methods shown in the accompanying illustrations is to close the opening in the pipe.

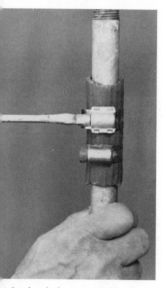

Seal a hole in a pipe using a section of water hose and two automotive clamps.

Pipe leak closed with moldable epoxy (right). Wipe area perfectly dry and roughen with sandpaper or steel wool before applying the epoxy. Warm to speed hardening.

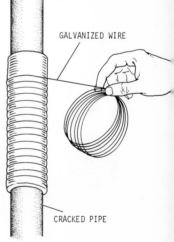

Another way to close a leak in a pipe carrying water under pressure is to wrap rubber, soft plastic, or leather around the pipe. Then, close-wind galvanized wire around the pipe for several inches over the hole.

PIPES, FROZEN

Protecting pipes. When the forecast warns of subnormal temperatures there are a number of steps you can take to prevent exposed water pipes from freezing. There is no need to protect soil pipes.

You can insulate the pipes passing near cellar windows or through uninsulated crawl spaces by wrapping them with strips of cloth, layers of newspapers, or cardboard held in place with wire or string.

You can raise the temperature of the pipe by wiring a soldering or pressing iron to it and plugging the iron in during the ultracold period. You can provide heat by attaching an electric light bulb to the pipe with layers of aluminum foil, and, of course, turning the light on when the cold wave hits.

You can open the faucet connected to the exposed pipe and let the water run all night. Moving water doesn't freeze as readily as still water.

You can also drain the water from the pipe. Obviously this is the only certain way of preventing the water in the pipe from freezing. To drain the pipe, close the valve leading to the pipe or pipes, open the faucets at the ends of the pipes and then open the drain cock, if there is one. In some of the colder areas of our country, shutoff valves and drain valves or drain cocks are part of the original plumbing system. Where there is no drain cock you can open the pipe line by unscrewing it, if it is a threaded pipe, or open it by unsoldering the joint if it is a soldered copper pipe system. You can also drive a nail through the copper pipe near the shutoff valve. This will, of course, drain the pipe. Then, when you have time, you can install a tap-on valve directly over the hole in the pipe. The tap-on valve is clamped in place. The only tool you need is a screwdriver. This done you can open and drain the pipe line any time you wish by just operating the valve.

One method of keeping water in a pipe from freezing is to wire a pressing iron to the pipe and turn on the iron.

When unthawing water in a pipe, always start at the end of the pipe so there is no possibility of steam pressure building up inside. To avoid damaging the washer and stem packing, remove the stem from the faucet or valve you are heating.

Frozen pipe. Let us suppose you have opened a faucet from whence water normally issues and nothing comes out. Since the temperature has gone far below normal, you know the water in the pipe is frozen. The question that needs to be answered at this point is, should you go to work and unthaw the pipe or should you wait till warmer weather?

If the temperature is going to remain much the same or become warmer, there is no need to tackle the tedious and difficult job of melting the ice in the pipes now. Whatever damage the frost is going to do it has already done—unless the temperature drops farther down. Pure water that is unconfined freezes at 32° F and expands approximately 11 percent. If water is confined as in a closed pipe where it cannot easily expand, its freezing point drops. Thus, if the pipe has not burst or cracked so far and the temperature has been low for an extended period of time, nothing will happen if the temperature doesn't drop further.

At the same time, there is no point in thawing a frozen pipe if there is the possibility of another cold spell and you have no way of draining that pipe or otherwise protecting it.

Let us consider another situation. The frost has cracked a pipe or valve. Thawing the pipe now will not save anything. The only reason for doing so (other than to remove and replace it) is to release the water while you are present and able to catch it.

Thawing a frozen pipe. There are a number of ways to thaw a frozen pipe, but whatever method you use you must *always start from the faucet.* The reason is simple enough. If you heat the pipe in the middle and its ends are closed you can develop sufficient steam pressure to blow the pipe open. So start by applying heat first to a faucet until you can turn the faucet to its open position and water drips out. Then work your way back up or down the pipe as the case may be. If the water stops dripping out of the faucet after you have moved the heat several feet farther along the pipe there is a chance the water has refrozen behind you. Bring the heat back to the faucet and start again. If it isn't too much trouble, unscrew the faucet, thereby speeding the flow of water out of the pipe.

The best means of heating a frozen pipe is a propane torch. Lacking that you can hold a large soldering iron or a pressing iron firmly against the pipe; you can wrap a towel around the pipe and pour boiling water on it; and you can even place a small electric stove beneath it. All the methods work, but not as fast as a torch.

PORCH

Floor damaged. Exposed to the weather and foot traffic as they are, porch floorboards wear out and break up. When you have suitable replacement lumber the job is simple carpentry. When you do not have proper replacement lumber available, you can make a strong, temporary repair with metal or wood.

Let the old board remain in place and nail a flat sheet of metal over the damaged or missing portion of the floor. Since the load on the metal results in a pulling, or tensile, action, any thin piece of metal large enough will do. You can even cut open a tin can, flatten it and nail it in place.

If you cannot secure a metal patch, bevel the edges of a thin board and nail that in place. The board is not as good as the metal because the board's edge can cause someone to stumble; still it is a lot better than stepping down through the porch floor.

Floor sags. A porch floor will sag for one or two reasons: A pier has crumbled or sunk some distance into the earth or a girder or joist has rotted. In both cases the immediate problem is to raise the porch floor back to its original height and to hold it there while repairs can be made.

The best means of raising a porch floor is a house jack. If you can rent one, place it on a 2 x 8 plank beneath the porch girder. Then extend the jack until the porch is back at the desired level. If the girder is too rotted to be lifted directly, or if you have to position the jack under joists attached to the girder, place a short plank on top of the jack to distribute the upward pressure.

If you cannot secure a house jack you can improvise a jack from pipe, timbers, wedges, and concrete block. And if the porch is not too heavy you can sometimes lift it with an automobile jack.

To make a pipe jack, you need several short lengths of threaded, galvanized pipe 1½ inches in diameter or larger, a sufficient number of couplings to join the pieces of pipe, two large Stillson wrenches, and a little oil or pipe cement. The more pieces of pipe and couplings you use the better. When the pipe is screwed all the way into the couplings, the total overall length of the pipe and couplings should be less than the distance from the top of the plank (or concrete block) you are going to use as a support to the bottom of the girder to be lifted.

Apply oil or pipe dope to the pipe threads. Make all the pipe hand tight in the couplings. Position the assembled pipes and couplings vertically beneath the girder. Unscrew the pipes from their couplings as far as they will go by hand. Now put the wrenches to them and open (expand) each joint a little until you have lifted the girder as far as you wish.

To form a wedge jack, place a plank beneath your porch as previously described.

A powerful jack can be made from several sections of pipe, nipples, and pipe couplings. The lift is secured when the pipe and couplings are unscrewed.

Cut a 4 x 4 a fraction of an inch shorter than the distance from the top of the plank to the underside of the girder. Position the 4 x 4 vertically and directly beneath the girder. Now drive wedges between the bottom of the 4 x 4 and the plank. Next, drive wedges between the top of the 4 x 4 and the bottom of the girder. If doing all this raises the girder to the necessary height, drive nails into the wedges to hold them in place until you can make a proper repair. If you still need to bring your porch up farther, cut a second 4 x 4. Fit that alongside the first and use more wedges to lift the porch. This will release the first 4 x 4, whereupon you can raise it with a wood spacer and use the wedges to go higher still. In this way, working from one 4 x 4 to another you can raise a porch or similar structure a considerable distance.

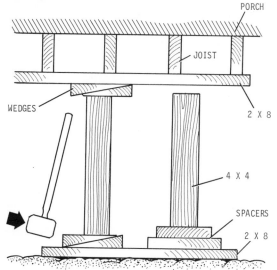

How a jack can be made from timbers and wedges. In use the wedges are used to lift the porch high enough to slip spacers beneath the second vertical timber. Then the wedges are used to lift the porch above the second timber while spacers are placed beneath the first.

Using an auto jack to raise a sagging porch.

If you don't have 4 x 4s or similar timbers you can do the same with concrete blocks piled atop one another.

A scissor-type jack can be used by raising it on concrete blocks so that it can reach the girder. A bumper-type jack may also be raised so that its arm can reach the underside of the girder. However, whereas a scissor jack is reasonably safe for this application, a bumper jack is not. You must fasten it to the side of the porch securely otherwise it will bend a little under the load and snap outwards from under the girder. At this instant it moves like a bullet and its action can be lethal. So wire and nail it to the side of the porch and stand clear when you operate the jack's handle.

Rail damaged. Lengthwise cracks in a wood rail can be quickly repaired by applying epoxy cement to the facing surfaces within the crack and then clamping the parts of the joint together by wrapping rope or string around it.

Where the end of a rail has rotted away next to the newel, cut the rail back as necessary and then nail a wood spacer to the side of the newel. The end of the rail can now be nailed to the spacer.

Another method consists of drilling a hole through the width of the rail and a parallel hole through the newel. This done, you can fasten the rail to the newel by lacing wire through the two holes and twisting the ends of the wire. It isn't neat, but it is strong and fast.

The same method can be used to join two parts of an iron railing that have come apart, generally at a defective weld. Drill a hole down through the rail and another through the newel or another portion of the rail. Then lace the two parts together with wire. Of course, if you have a piece of strap iron and some nuts and bolts, you can make the repair that way.

Loose posts can be tightened by pounding lead into the space between the post and the concrete, assuming the concrete is not broken. If the concrete is broken, join the pieces with epoxy. Another possibility is to wet the pieces of concrete and the slab and then join the pieces with a mixture of cement and sand. Use 1 part cement to 2 parts sand and sufficient water to make a soft paste. Assemble and hold all the parts and the rail immobile for at least a week. After the first two days, keep the cement wet to help it harden.

Roof sags. If possible rent an adjustable lally column. This is a house jack built into the end of a strong pipe. Use it to raise the sagging porch roof and hold it there until you can make repairs.

If an adjustable lally column is not available and the sag amounts to no more than a few inches, place a plank beneath the porch at the point of greatest roof sag. Position the plank so that one fourth of its length is beneath the porch and the rest projects away from the side of the porch. Cut a 4 x 4 (or nail two 2 x 4s together) to a length that is equal to the distance from the underside of the porch roof at its low point to the surface of the plank, plus 3 or 4 inches.

Position the 4 x 4 between the under edge of the porch roof at its low point and the surface of the plank. Now drive the bottom end of the 4 x 4 towards the porch. Since the 4 x 4 is at an angle, driving it into a vertical position raises its top end. In this way you will be able to lift the sagging roof. If the roof is very heavy, you may have to use two or more angled 4 x 4s to do the job. Once you have lifted the roof to its designed height, nail one end of the 4 x 4 to the roof and the other to the plank to hold it in place.

Steps damaged. Back-porch and similarly exposed wooden steps frequently rot, especially where the treads contact the stringer. In such cases it isn't enough, from the point of view of safety, to merely drive a few more nails through the tread and into the stringer. The wiser emergency repair consists of nailing a 2 x 6 along the inside of each stringer first. In this way you can be reasonably certain the stringers are not going to give way on you. Where necessary you can indent the 2 x 6s so as to better support the treads.

The proper way to repair a cracked stringer, other than by replacing it, is to nail a piece of 2x6 over the weak area.

POWER FAILURE

Turn off or disconnect all the electrical motors in your home. Refrigerators and freezers can be turned off by turning their temperature controls back to zero. The oil burner motor can be prevented from going on by turning the heat back to 45° F. Other motors can be similarly treated or disconnected. The reason for this is that in many instances when power is restored it is far below normal voltage for a period of time. When an electrical motor is operated at much less than its rated voltage it may burn out because it cannot switch from its starting coil to its running coil.

Do not assume that the voltage is correct when power is restored by judging from the brightness of your lights. Your eye cannot do this accurately. Phone the power company or the police to make certain it is safe to operate your motors again.

Take immediate steps to conserve whatever heat or cold you may have. If it is winter, close all the windows, lower the storms into place. Move into one room, preferably over the heating system.

To conserve cold, do not open the freezer or refrigerator any more than you have to. Do not remove ice cubes nor try to make additional ice. Generally a refrigerator will hold food safely cool for 24 hours; a freezer will do the same for about 48 hours.

If the power is off a long time and you believe the interior of your home will go below freezing, provide auxiliary heat, shut and drain the water from all the pipes, but only after the water in the pipes has become really cold. A lukewarm radiator still throws a little heat. There is no point in wasting it.

PUMP, SUMP

Noisy. The pump may be worn, and its parts may be loose. It is best to repair the pump as soon as possible, but let it continue to run if the cellar is flooding. The pump itself may be satisfactory. The trouble may be due to a partially clogged discharge line or a partially clogged directional valve in the line. The valve itself may be worn and chattering.

Won't start. Check for power. If power is present, try lifting the float manually. It may be jammed in the down (off) position by debris or the float ball may be waterlogged. Operate the float manually until you have time for proper repairs.

Won't stop. The float may be stuck in the up (on) position. Try pushing it down. In some designs the float is connected to the switch by a wire cable. See that the cable is not caught in the opening. Then check whether the discharge pipe is clogged, in which case the pump cannot force the water out of the sump as fast as additional water seeps in, so that the pump operates continuously. To make this check, turn the pump off and watch the water level in the sump. If the level does not rise or rises at a very slow rate that can easily be accommodated by the pump the fault lies in the discharge line.

Test the control rod and float on a sump pump for freedom of movement by lifting it up and down. To vary the water level at which the pump goes on and off, adjust the rod in relation to the switch. If the pump does not run, try shorting the switch (be sure to disconnect the pump). That may permit you to operate the pump.

RADIO, PORTABLE

If the sound is low and distorted, this is almost always due to a weak battery. Replace the battery. If you have no replacement, remove the battery and let it rest and warm up for an hour or more. It then should have sufficient power to operate the receiver for a while.

If your receiver has individual dry cells, remove them and punch small holes in their sides. Then place the cells, positive connection up, in a dish filled with a solution of salt and water. The solution should not cover the cells. Let the cells remain for an hour or two. Remove and dry them. Then wrap them in adhesive tape and replace them in the receiver. All this will give the cells additional power, and you should be able to secure satisfactory reception for a short while.

RANGE, ELECTRIC

If none of the elements heat up, the trouble is a blown fuse or an open circuit breaker. If one or more elements heat up, the range is receiving electric power and the remaining elements (or their associated switches) are defective. There is no harm in using an element that is partially burned out; all you are doing is using a piece of it. However, if the element is so far gone that you can see the internal heating wire, *do not use it.* Under the right (or wrong) conditions the cook can receive the full voltage delivered to the range, so don't take chances.

One cause of trouble on an electric range is sticking pushbutton switches. Loosen them by spraying with a TV switch-cleaning solution.

When an element appears to be in good condition but you can only get it to partially heat up, the trouble may be due to the switch. If your range has push buttons, they may be sticking and not making contact. Try pouring a little of the switch-cleaning fluid sold for cleaning TV receiver switches down into the buttons. This can loosen them.

If element operation is still unsatisfactory after releasing the switch buttons, don't waste your time looking for loose wires. You won't find any. The elements and/or switches have to be replaced, which means you need new parts to do the job. It is not difficult; just change one wire at a time so that you do not mix them up.

Incidentally, the life of the exposed electric range elements is greatly reduced by water. When a pot overflows and the liquid hits the red-hot element it corrodes it at a tremendous rate.

RANGE, GAS

Pilot light will not remain on. Make certain the room is well ventilated and that gas has not collected in and near the range. Look beneath the front gas manifold—the pipe into which all the individual burner pipes are connected—in line with the small tube leading to the pilot light for a small setscrew. Backing this screw out half a turn or so increases the flow of gas to the pilot light. The light should be about ½ inch high for the best compromise between gas saving and a sturdy flame.

Pilot will not light burners. If the pilot is on but the burners do not ignite by themselves when you open their valves, the trouble could be due to an undersized pilot-light flame. It can also be caused by a clogged ignition pipe leading from the pilot to the burner jets. Another cause is clogged holes in the burner jets near the ignition pipe. Still another could be a maladjusted air valve on that particular burner. See the following section.

The size of the pilot-light flame can be increased as explained above. The ignition tube can be cleaned by poking it clear with a stiff wire. To remove the tube, lift the iron grillwork up and out of the way and then just pull the tube up. The holes in the burner can be cleaned by poking them open with a stiff wire. For a better and more complete cleaning, remove the grill. Pull the burner rearward and then up and out. Then place the cast-iron burner in boiling water to which a little lye or strong soap has been added. This cleans and degreases the burner.

Gas burns yellow, pots get sooty. This means the gas flame isn't getting sufficient air. At the end of the burner casting where it enters the manifold you will see a little rotary slide valve. Loosen the setscrew. Slide the valve plate around until the gas burns blue and makes a slight hissing noise. Tighten the screw and the adjustment is done.

Loose gas valve. When the size of the gas flame increases or decreases by itself, the trouble is usually a loose gas valve. The cure is to tighten the screw you will find on the end of the valve shaft.

RECORD PLAYER

Won't start. Check the wall outlet for power. Spin the record by hand. It may have stopped in an in-between position when someone turned it off, and the record will not start automatically until its mechanism is past that position.

Tone arm slides off the record. This is usually due to a worn needle. Tape a dime to the middle of the arm. The extra weight on the needle doesn't do the record any good, but it does reduce the arm's side movement.

Sounds strange. Most likely the turntable is revolving at a speed other than the one for which the record was designed. Vary the speed control.

Very loud hum. If the hum increases tremendously as your hand approaches the pickup arm, the trouble is an open connection between the pickup arm and the amplifier. Shut the unit off and look for the broken connection on the underside of the pickup arm.

REFRIGERATOR. see FREEZER

ROOF

Chimney leaks. Leaks between the roof and the chimney are usually due to either the upper edges of the flashing coming loose from the side of the chimney or the flashing disintegrating, usually at the bend where the roof meets the chimney.

The upper edges of the flashing can sometimes be repositioned with short nails driven through the flashing and into the mortar. Then the joint is sealed with asphalt applied with a small stick.

When the flashing is breaking into two pieces at the joint between the roof and the chimney you can sometimes seal the joint with asphalt applied to the corner after you have lifted the shingles up and out of the way. A better way consists of slipping new pieces of flashing beneath the old and holding them in place with a drop of asphalt until you have time to do the job properly. As an alternative to metal pieces of flashing you can use pieces of asphalt roofing shingles cut to size. These have to be thoroughly warmed before bending otherwise they will crack. Still another method consists of applying a thick bead of asphalt to the joint between the roof and the chimney. The trouble with this method is that it results in a large black band, and in hot weather the asphalt tends to run.

Flat roof leaks. If you can find a section of roof covering that has bubbled up in response to heat and underlying moisture and has broken, cut the bubble, spread a layer of asphalt over it and then nail a piece of asphalt roof shingle or 30-pound saturated felt over it. If you have no shingle or felt, the asphalt alone will hold for a while.

If you can find no openings of any kind, the leakage is due to a general deterioration of the roof covering. Thousands of tiny holes have developed, all of which pass water. There is no easy repair. You have to completely recover this roof.

Pitched roof leaks. To make an exterior repair, find the hole, slip a good shingle under the next-highest shingle on the roof. A couple of nails will hold it in place. Since your new shingle covers the hole and its upper edge is beneath an old shingle, water will roll over the hole in the roof without trouble.

To carry out an interior repair, find the hole. This may not be easy since the drip may be several feet lower than the actual hole. Smear a layer of tar over the hole and the adjoining underside of the roof. Cut a board to match the space between the rafters. Place it tightly against the hole and nail it to the rafters. Hopefully, the tar will seal the space between the board and the underside of the roof. In any event, whether or not a perfect seal is made, this patch will greatly reduce rain water coming through a bad hole in the roof.

Vent pipe leaks. For an interior repair, assuming you can reach the vent pipe where it passes through the roof, wrap several turns of a rag around the pipe, just as high as you can reach. With a small stick, cover the upper surfaces of the rag with asphalt. Then push the cloth ring up the length of the pipe and against the underside of the roof.

If the leak is an exterior one between the flashing and the pipe, seal the joint with asphalt. If you have no asphalt you can use masking or adhesive tape. It will hold for a while. If the leak is between the flashing and a shingle, follow the suggestion for temporarily installing a shingle on a pitched roof given previously.

To stop a leak in a roof without going outside, nail a board to the underside of the roof. Use cleats or toenail into the rafters, not the roof boards.

SEPTIC TANK

Septic tanks depend upon the action of anaerobic bacteria converting much of the solid waste into a liquid in the tank itself and upon aerobic bacteria converting the effluent (liquid that flows out of the tank) into harmless substances.

Odor. If the drain field (surface) is dry, the trouble may be due to a loose septic tank cover, which should be tightened. It may also be caused by a brief warm spell in the middle of winter. The aerobic bacteria are inactivated by the cold, which does not result in an odor when the ground is frozen. But when the earth is thawed suddenly and briefly an odor is produced by the untreated effluent. Nothing can be done about this. Do not cover the drain field with more soil. To do this would further reduce the activity of the aerobic bacteria, as they need air to function.

If the drain field is wet, the excess water prevents the bacteria from receiving the air they require. Consequently the effluent is untreated and an odor results. Reduce the quantity of water that may be used by your family. Cut shower time and the number of baths taken per day. If possible, reconnect the drainpipe leading out of the dishwasher and clothes washer to a dry well. If any of your house leaders are draining into the house drain system, disconnect them. Too much water in the tank will always interfere with proper bacterial action.

Sluggish action. If the house drainpipe acts as if it is partially clogged, open the septic tank. If its surface is covered with coagulated grease, you can try dissolving that grease with sulfuric acid. Purchase a gallon or two of the concentrated acid in a plumbing supply shop. It is sold under various trade names such as Clobber, Bust-Loose, etc. Be certain to wear rubber gloves when you handle the acid and to pour very slowly: you don't want to splash. Generally, dissolving the grease in the tank speeds its action.

Plugged sewer line. If your sewer line plugs up and running a snake down to its end (the T in the septic tank) doesn't open the line, there is a good chance the blockage is due to an accumulation of either detergent or kitchen grease at the T fitting which terminates the sewer line. To get to this fitting, remove the tank's cover and reach in with a bent iron rod or a length of strap iron. All you need do is push the hardened material out of the way.

SEWER-PIPE STOPPAGES

Stoppages in the sewer pipe or the house drain, which is what the sewer pipe is called while it is still in the building, are reasonably easy to clear when you have a suitable snake. If you have no snake your success or failure will depend on the location of the stoppage and its nature. If the stoppage is limited to the house trap, you can probably clear it with a piece of wire. If it lies in the house drain or in the sewer line and is soft you can possibly clear it using a garden hose.

Locating the point of blockage. If possible, wait until early morning. That will give the system time to drain and reduce the chance of a flood when you open the pipe. Remove the highest cleanout plug first. If you do not have a wrench of a suitable size, tap the edge of the plug with a chisel and a hammer to turn it around. If, on removing the highest cleanout plug, you encounter water, push the snake through the opening and down the drainpipe until you clear the obstruction or cannot force the snake to go any farther. The usual method when urging on a snake (or a garden hose substitute) is to turn it as you give it a series of forward pushes.

When seeking the cause of stoppage in the house drain and sewer pipe, start by opening the highest cleanout in the drain system. This will reduce the chance of a flood.

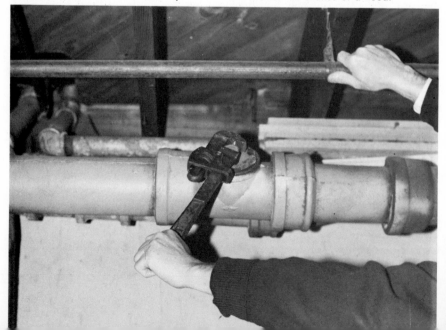

Always open the side of the trap nearest the sewer side of the pipe first. When the plugs are embedded in lead, as these are, they have to be knocked out rather than unscrewed. To replace them, pound them back into the trap.

When you do not have a suitable snake, you can sometimes make do with a water hose. Keep poking it into the pipe until you push the obstruction out of the way.

If you do not encounter water at the highest cleanout, go to the next and try again. There may be a second, lower cleanout. If not, the next plug to remove is that on the sewer side of the house trap (the large U-shaped pipe close to the cellar wall). If you find water there the blockage lies in the pipe leading from the trap to the city sewer or your septic tank. Push the snake through the trap opening towards the city sewer as far as you can. If you can break the blockage the water will drain out of the pipe. As stated previously, if you have a long, strong snake or you are using a garden hose and the blockage is soft, it is just a matter of pushing the material out of the way.

If, on opening the side of the trap closest to the cellar wall, you find the usual quantity of water in the bottom of the trap, the trouble is higher up the drainpipe. First, use the snake or a piece of stiff wire to slowly and carefully make certain the trap itself is not clogged. This ascertained or corrected, remove the second plug from the trap. Now poke the snake slowly up the drainpipe. This is another common trouble spot, and if there is water behind the blockage, you certainly do not want to release it all at once, so work carefully.

If and when you have found the blockage, check your work by flushing one clean toilet and watching the water flow with a flashlight directed into the trap.

SHOWER, STALL

Won't drain. Some shower drains lead to drum traps. If this is the kind your shower has, the plumbing code requires that it must be accessible. Look for it behind a trap door in a nearby closet. If there is one and you can find it, it is generally not difficult to remove its cover, and then cleaning is very simple. Cleaning the trap out, will of course, open up the shower drainpipe.

If that is not possible, try poking a wire or the end of a garden hose down the drain, after you have removed the safety screen above the drain opening.

SINK, BATHROOM

Bathroom sinks are subject to the same ills as kitchen sinks, with the added problem of hair accumulations.

Won't drain. Place a bucket beneath the trap under the basin. Remove the large plug (nut) you find there. Bend a little hook in the end of a length of stiff wire, and with this remove the debris that has collected in the trap and is preventing the passage of water.

If you can't remove the plug (there may not be one), remove the entire trap, if possible. If this too is impossible, try poking a hooked wire down through the drainpipe. (Wire cut from a clothes hanger will do fine.) If this fails to get results, you can resort to the boiling-water treatment, but since most bathroom sinks become clogged with hair as much as with soap and grease, do not expect too much from the boiling water.

Drainpipe leaks. In addition to leaks at the joints which can be treated exactly the same way as that suggested for treating drainpipe leaks in kitchen sinks (see SINK, KITCHEN), bathroom sinks sometimes leak through the ball and socket joint that is part of the stopper mechanism. If this is the case, try tightening the collar. If that doesn't stop the leaking, remove the collar and place a little putty between the ball and its seat. When you replace the collar the putty will hold the water in until you can secure the proper replacement gasket and install it.

Stopper won't hold water. Lift the stopper and remove any foreign material that may have collected beneath it, preventing a proper seal. If the stopper has a rubber gasket and it is damaged or worn, there is nothing you can do except replace the gasket. On the other hand if the gasket is satisfactory, and the seat is clean, the trouble is due to the levers actuating the stopper, which are holding the stopper clear of its seat. Trace the levers and adjust as necessary.

Stopper cannot be lifted. This may be caused by improperly adjusted levers or worn lever supports. In the latter case, try bending the levers.

Cracked or broken. Cracked or broken porcelain sinks can be repaired by carefully drying all the pieces and all the broken edges. Then epoxy cement is spread

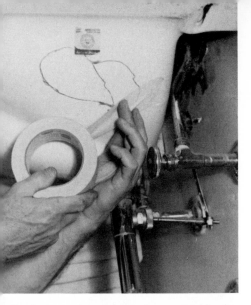

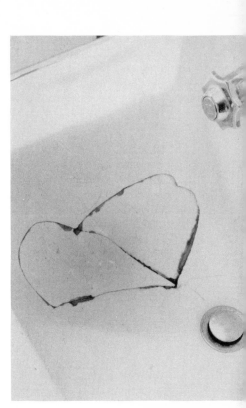

Cracked porcelain sinks can be repaired by drying and coating the pieces with epoxy. Hold the parts in place with masking tape. The finished job is not beautiful, but it will hold for years, or until you can replace the sink.

over the broken edges and forced into the cracks. Next, the pieces are reassembled using adhesive or masking tape to hold them together, plus pieces of wood as props if necessary. When thoroughly dry, the sink can be used again. Carefully cemented, it will hold together this way for years.

SINK, KITCHEN

Drainpipe leaks. First, try tightening the large flange nuts on the drainpipe. They do not have to be very tight to hold; even finger tight will do when the gasket underneath is in good condition. However, if you can't stop the leak with your fingers alone, use a large wrench. (See TOOLS if you haven't got one.) However, no matter what kind of a wrench you may use, take care not to overtighten the flange nut, as you can easily rip an old pipe apart.

If tightening the flange nut doesn't stop the leaking, the gasket is at fault. Back the nut off. Remove the gasket and replace it with several turns of heavy string that has been coated with wax.

As an alternative you can dry the flange nut and adjoining pipes and seal the joint with epoxy cement or with wet plaster backed with a strip of cloth.

A plumber's poultice: wet plaster smeared over a strip of cloth. This will hold for many years, but only on drainpipes.

Spray works poorly. This may be caused by grit in the filter at the end of the faucet spout. Unscrew the filter, clean it and replace it. The trouble may also be due to grit in the spray head, which should be disassembled and cleaned as necessary.

Won't drain. If there is no movement of the water at all, remove as much as you can with a sponge, then disassemble the trap (curved pipe) beneath the sink. If you do not have a suitable snake on hand, try poking a garden hose or a wire with a hook bent into its end down the sink's drain.

Wait until all the water has flowed out of the sink and then pour boiling water down the drain. Repeat this as many times as necessary. Since most kitchen sinks become plugged with kitchen grease, hot water, when it can pass through, will carry some of the grease along with it.

TABLES

Legs are loose. Many table legs are bolted to a cleat fastened with screws and glue to the underside of the table top. Tighten the wood screws and the nut to tighten the leg. If the bolt itself (a hanger bolt with a screw at one end) is loose, back the nut off and with a pair of pliers, turn the bolt clockwise to drive its screw end back into the wood. Then tighten the nut.

Table halves won't separate. Lie on your back directly beneath the table. Place the bottoms of your feet on the underside of one edge of the table and your hands on the underside of the opposite edge. Now push. By positioning yourself this way, you can exert a lot more force in the necessary direction than you can by leaning over the table and trying to pull its halves apart.

Table halves won't close on leaf. This may be due to grime in the holes in the facing edges of the two table halves. Clean them out. It may also be due to a warped leaf. Position the leaf and then have someone stand on the leaf, with their feet on the high points, while you press the table halves together.

TELEPHONE

Even though the youngest in your home may know how to use the telephone few adults, let alone children, know how to use it properly to call for help, and even fewer homes have emergency phone numbers posted alongside each telephone.

The proper way to call for help is to state your name, address, and problem in that order. Most police officers answering your call will not accept any information until they have your name and address. This firm rule results from the practice of many excited individuals to call and say, "My house is on fire. Help," and hang up. Obviously, your information is worthless unless they know where you are. The request for identification is made to discourage crank calls.

Your phone number list should have the local police number on top. They will respond most quickly. This should be followed by the fire department, doctor, hospital, dependable friend, and other important telephone numbers.

Take the time to acquaint your family with the presence of these numbers and to teach the youngsters the proper procedure in calling for help. Have them make a few practice emergency phone calls to be certain they have it right.

TELEVISION

Set won't go on. Check the wall outlet to make certain there is power there. Examine the back of the receiver to make certain it is properly in place. Many TV receivers have a safety switch built into their back cover. If the cover is removed or not properly replaced the set will not go on. Look for a small cartridge fuse beneath a plastic screw cap. If there is a fuse and it is burned out cover the fuse with foil if you do not have a replacement. That will get you running again.

Poor picture. If the picture is poor on all channels, this is possibly caused by a defective antenna. Place a finger on one antenna terminal. If the picture improves, try disconnecting one antenna wire and connecting a short piece of wire to one antenna connection. (You can also climb onto the roof and find the break in the TV lead-in wire.)

If the picture is very poor on one channel, try adjusting the fine tuning when you are tuned to that channel. Also try switching to an adjacent channel and adjusting the fine tuning there to get the station you want.

If the picture is good only when you are switching from one channel to the next, the channel switch contacts are dirty. Try to adjust the switch so that it remains between stations for at least the length of your favorite program. A pos-

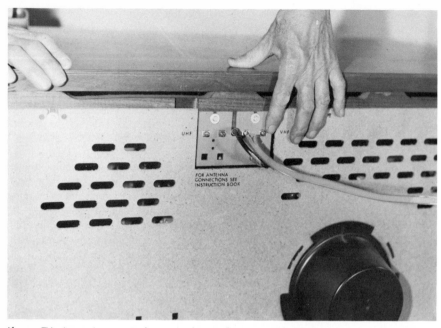

If your TV picture improves when you place a finger on either antenna connection, chances are your antenna system—lead wires or antenna—is defective.

sible cure consists of squirting a switch-cleaning solution into the switch. You can purchase this solvent in a radio supply shop. Instructions are to be found on the container.

If the color is poor, try varying the color controls. If the color is still poor the chances are that the antenna is defective (fallen down, broken lead, corrosion). Color receivers require a comparatively strong signal to function properly.

In the case of a dark picture, the trouble is due to a worn picture tube. Purchase a booster at a radio supply shop. This is a little transformer that increases the voltage to the picture tube, making it brighter.

Poor sound. Try adjusting the fine tuning.

TERMITES

The presence of termites in your home may come to your attention in any of three ways. You may see what appears to be a large number of ants flying about your home in the spring or early summer. You may see half-round tunnels of mud constructed on the side of your foundation wall, leading from the earth to the wooden portion of the building. You may suddenly find some seemingly solid portion of your home breaking under your hand or foot.

The fact that there are some forty known varieties of termites in the United States, that the point of greatest infestation is believed to be Southern Mississippi, that only the blind workers rip into wood—all this is of small importance to you. When you encounter evidence of termite activity you should immediately engage in counteractivity to prevent further damage and to prevent their numbers from increasing.

Destroying the termites. Start by destroying all the termite tunnels. If you have an earth floor beneath the building, as for example in a crawl space, be certain to inspect the walls there. Then dig a trench alongside the foundation of your building. Make the trench about 1 foot wide and 2 feet deep. Do the same alongside the inside of all foundation walls adjoining a dirt floor. Remove whatever rotted pieces of wood you may encounter while digging the trench, and remove whatever wood may be piled near the building, as for example fireplace logs.

The next step is to purchase a quantity of chlordan and mix it with water following the directions. Pour the mixture into the trenches you have dug. Be very careful with this chemical; it is a powerful poison. Replace the soil. The chlordan will prevent termites from breeding in the earth alongside your home for many years.

Further preventive measures. When you replace the soil in the trench alongside your home's foundation, relandscape the area so that there is a span of at least 18 inches between the surface of the soil and the lowest building timbers. This will not prevent termites from constructing tunnels on the foundation wall and attacking the timbers, but it will definitely slow them down.

Cover all your interior earth floors with either a layer of concrete or asphalt. Neither need be very thick.

If you have wooden outbuildings that rest directly on the earth, remove the buildings or lift them up the suggested 18 inches. Wood resting on soil provides a natural home for termites. When their numbers grow they will move on to other buildings. Remember, they fly during mating season.

Repairing damage. At this point you are more or less assured your home will not be further troubled by termites. However, if their damage is already extensive, you must find it before the house sags and cracks and do something to replace or strengthen the weakened timbers.

To find termite-damaged timber try to poke the end of an ice pick into the wood. If you can force the point more than ½ inch into the wood, the termites have been feasting there. Let the damaged timber be and place a reinforcing timber alongside. Then nail the new timber to the old. If you do this quickly enough you will prevent the building from sagging, which will necessitate lifting the building and repairing the cracks.

TILES, CERAMIC

Cracked tiles can be left in place and the cracks filled with a little plaster of Paris. A fallen tile should be returned to its place as soon as possible to prevent water from getting behind the other tiles and loosening them.

Generally, you will find it almost impossible to return the fallen tile to its position without enlarging the original space. This may be done with a small cold chisel and a hammer or with an old screwdriver in place of the chisel. Be certain to tap the chisel gently so as not to·loosen the balance of the tiles and crack the supporting masonry.

When you have removed sufficient mortar to permit the tile to be returned to its position, soak the tile in water and then cement it in place with a little wet plaster of Paris. Wipe the excess plaster off with a sponge.

If the tile is supported by Sheetrock (plasterboard), scrape the old adhesive off with a chisel. Wet the tile and cement it back in place with plaster.

TOASTER

Doesn't heat. Check the wall outlet for power. Another appliance may have blown the kitchen fuse or the fuse that powers some of the kitchen's electrical outlets. Examine the plug on the end of the line cord to see that the wires aren't disconnected. If neither of these steps uncovers the cause of the malfunction, remove the toaster plug from the wall. Turn the toaster over, brush all the bread crumbs out. Shake the toaster vigorously to get the unreachable crumbs out. Sometimes pieces of bread interfere with the toaster's internal switch mechanism.

All crumbs removed, try the toaster again. If it still doesn't function, remove the plug again and inspect the heating element wires for a break. Assuming that there is a break in the heating wires and that you can find it, use a piece of clean, bare copper wire to join the ends. Usually the heater wire itself is too brittle to bend into a joint. The copper jumper should give you several dozen slices of toast before it too breaks down.

Overtoasts. This is caused by an inoperative timing switch. If you have already turned the control switch all the way to light, turn the machine over and examine its bottom. Some designs have a second timing switch on their bottoms. Adjust this and see what happens. If the toaster still remains on too long, disconnect it from the wall outlet, let it cool and examine its insides. Look for crumbs or carbonized jelly, sugar, and the like (from toasting cake) that may have fallen on the timing mechanism, not necessarily locking it, but insulating it so that it remains comparatively cool. Scrape it clean. Sometimes the screws holding parts of the thermostatic switch to the bottom of the toaster are loose. When this happens the switch is never as hot as the toaster and thus does not respond when it should. Tighten the screws.

Makes a buzzing sound. This is usually caused by a partially closed switch. Lift the switch arm and push it down again. If this doesn't stop the buzz, remove the toaster's plug from the wall outlet and clean out its insides. Crumbs may be preventing the switch from closing properly.

TOILET

Bowl won't drain. This is, of course, caused by a blockage in the drainpipe, but since the toilet itself has a trap, the most common stoppage trouble occurs here. A blockage at the toilet trap is not too difficult to remedy with the correct tools, which are a force pump (plunger) and/or a closet auger. Without these tools the job is messy to put it mildly; however, it can be done. You have to either pull the obstruction out of the toilet's trap or push it out of the trap and down into the drainpipe which is larger in diameter. Use a length of wire with a hook bent into its end or else a piece of garden hose.

If and when you believe you have removed the obstruction, try pouring a bucket of water carefully into the toilet bowl before you try flushing the toilet the usual way.

Doesn't flush fully. This is usually due to insufficient water in the tank. Remove the tank cover. If the level of the water is much less than 2 inches from the top of the tank, bend the rod attached to the ball so as to raise the position of the ball. That will permit more water to flow into the tank.

If there is plenty of water in the tank and yet the bowl is not completely cleaned with each flush, you probably have a partial blockage in the drain. Avoid flushing a second time while there is still water in the bowl. Doing so can cause the bowl to overflow. Remove the obstruction as soon as you can.

Doesn't stop running. Remove the cover from the tank. If water is entering the overflow pipe, bend the arm holding the float downward. Flush and wait. If that doesn't do it, lift the float firmly upwards. If the flow of water into the tank still persists, your ball-cock valve needs a new washer, and there is nothing to be done at this time except to close the valve in the pipe delivering water to the tank. You will find this valve under the tank.

If you find that the level of the water in the tank is not up to the top of the ball-cock valve, your trouble lies in the stopper ball or its attached wires. See that they are not bent and that the ball can rise and descend without getting stuck. If this is not the trouble, the ball is not seating properly. Let the ball descend and then turn it a few times as you press it into its seat. That should do it for the night. Next day you can scrub the seat and ball bottom smooth with steel wool.

Tank is cracked. Close the valve leading to the tank. Drain the tank completely of water. You will need a sponge to remove the water from the bottom of the tank. Dry the tank thoroughly by placing a toaster inside. Then force epoxy into the crack.

You can do the same with a cracked tank cover. To make the joint strong, reinforce it with a piece of metal or plastic.

Valve sings. A loud, vibratory noise every time the tank fills itself after being emptied is caused by a combination of high water pressure and a worn ball-cock valve. Reduce the pressure of the water entering the ball-cock valve by partially closing the valve leading to the tank.

TOOLS

Knife. Hacksaw steel is hard enough to take a good edge. Wrap tape around one end of a hacksaw blade to fashion a handle. Grind the nontoothed edge of the blade to knife sharpness. If the blade is too long for convenient use, bend it sharply and it will break.

Files are also made of high-temper steel. If you have a power grinder with which to cut the file down, it too makes an excellent knife.

Screwdriver. Dimes and other coins can be used in place of a conventional screwdriver when too much torque isn't required. If you can't turn the screw with your fingers alone, use a pair of pliers to help you. If you do not have pliers, clamp the coin or washer between two pieces of metal as shown.

Use a coin or washer in place of a screwdriver. When more torque is required than you can manage with fingers alone, hold the washer with a pair of pliers.

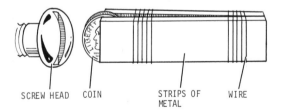

SCREW HEAD   COIN   STRIPS OF   WIRE
METAL

If you have no pliers, clamp the coin or washer between two strips of metal to make a screwdriver.

If the screwdriver you have is too large, grind it down. If its point is too thin to fit the screw-head slot properly, grind the point back.

If you cannot turn the screwdriver with your hands alone, put a crescent wrench on its shaft if the shaft is square. If the shaft is round, turn it with the aid of a small Stillson wrench.

A file can be ground into a screwdriver, if necessary. Grind the tang end down. To make a very small screwdriver, grind or file down the end of a nail file.

A rock tied to a stick is a Stone Age tool, but it still works well when you have nothing better.

Hammer. Any old rock will do as a hammer, but if you have to strike more than a few blows, or if you need a lot of striking power, attach a handle to the rock. One way this may be accomplished is shown in the photo.

Pliers. You can fashion a pair of noncutting pliers from a pair of sticks or pieces of metal and some wire. The resulting tool may not be convenient to use, but it will work. The homemade pliers in use is shown in an accompanying illustration.

Oversize wrench. You can sometimes make an oversize wrench fit a nut by placing a metal shim between the side of the wrench and the nut. When the space is large, use the tip of a screwdriver.

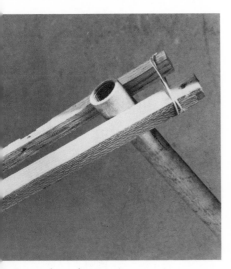

Two sticks and some wire or even rope can be used to make an effective pair of pliers.

When the wrench you have is too large for the nut, fill the space with the tip of a screwdriver or a piece of metal.

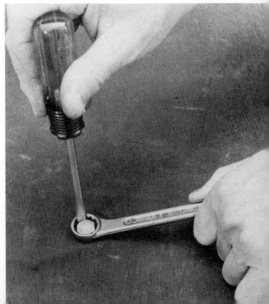

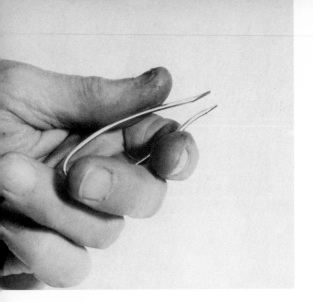

A pair of tweezers made from a fold of wire, sharpened to a flat point at the ends.

Undersize wrench. If a box wrench is just a mite small and you don't mind losing it, hacksaw a slot through the side of the box portion of the wrench. Now you can force the wrench over the nut and hopefully loosen or tighten the nut.

Chisel. You can use a screwdriver as it is as a cold chisel, or you can file or grind a point on it first. You can also convert a screwdriver into a wood chisel by filing or grinding a long, beveled point on its end.

File ends can be converted into wood chisels by similar grinding.

Tweezers. A pair of tweezers can be made from a bent piece of wire with its ends pounded or filed flat.

Clamps. You can make clamps from pieces of wood, wire, rope, or a long bolt and a nut. A few of the many possible arrangements are shown in the accompanying drawings.

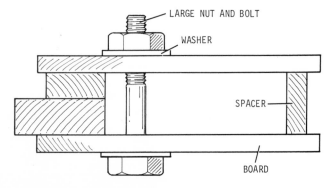

Clamp made from some boards and a large nut and bolt.

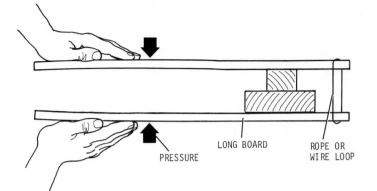

LONG BOARD

ROPE OR
WIRE LOOP

PRESSURE

Another clamp design made from boards and a loop of wire or rope. Wrap wire or rope around the ends of the clamp if you want the object to remain under pressure.

Vise. A vise can be rigged up from a pair of boards and a nut and bolt. A vise can also be made without a nut and bolt by using boards and wedges. See the accompanying drawings.

Sharpening. You can use a brick, a stone, or even the underside of an unglazed plate as a sharpening stone. Use any of these exactly as you would use a standard sharpening stone.

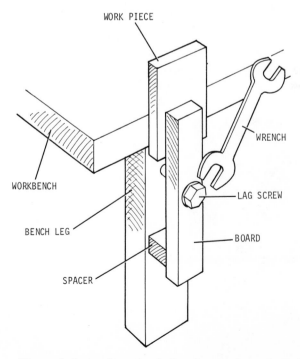

WORK PIECE

WRENCH

WORKBENCH

LAG SCREW

BENCH LEG

BOARD

SPACER

Vise made from a large lag bolt and some pieces of wood.

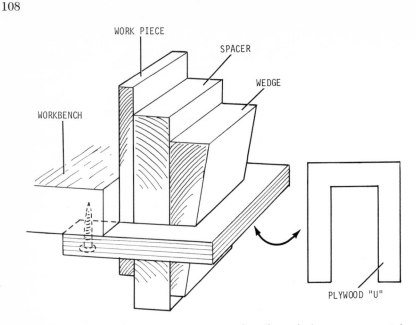

WORK PIECE

SPACER

WEDGE

WORKBENCH

PLYWOOD "U"

Wedge-type vise used many centuries ago and easily made from scrap materials.

Sandpaper. In the absence of sandpaper you can place a handful of sand on the object to be sanded, cover the sand with a small sponge or a folded cloth and sand away more or less as usual. If you must have a level surface, you can wrap a piece of cloth tightly around a block of wood, making certain the cloth on one side of the block is perfectly smooth. Then spread a smooth layer of Elmer's glue across the surface of the cloth. Cover the glue with sand and then press the sand into the glue with a second, flat piece of wood. When the glue dries you will have a sanding block you can use just like regular sandpaper.

Using a brick to sharpen a knife.

WATER, DRINKING

While we need both food and water to live, water is the more critical of the two since we cannot survive more than a few days without at least a quart of water per individual per day in cool weather. In hot weather we need more than twice this quantity and in a desert we need about a gallon of water per person. Therefore, if you live in an area that is completely dependent upon pipes or trucked-in water, be certain to store a goodly supply at all times, plus the means to purify the water.

Discontinued service. In the event of a possible shutdown of municipal water service you will probably be warned by radio or TV. In such cases fill whatever pots and pans you may have with water, even though you may also have additional stored water on hand. Cover the pots and place them in a cool place. If you have time, wash all your bath tubs carefully. Close their stoppers and fill them with water. Then close the main water valve in the basement. (This is done to prevent water you have in your pipes from flowing back into the city's main when the pressure is cut.) Next, close the valves leading to the toilet tanks; you can no longer afford the luxury of flushing your toilets.

If your water pressure dwindles to nothing without forewarning of a shutdown, (and you are connected to a city main), close the main valve in the basement and the valves leading to the toilet tanks. You now have the water that may be present in your pipes, and whatever you may collect elsewhere.

Utilizing the water in the house. The water in the house pipes can be secured by simply opening the faucets as usual. To speed flow, open partway both a hot and a cold faucet in a top-floor sink. Note that there is nothing wrong with drinking water that comes out of the hot-water tap. It is just as pure as water coming out of the cold-water tap.

When the water in the house water pipes has been used up, and you have a domestic hot-water boiler, you can utilize its water. First make certain you have an open hot-water faucet upstairs, then open the drain cock at the bottom of the hot-water tank and draw what you need.

When this is used up, and you have a hot-water heating system in your home,

Emptying a hot-water heating system of its water. The water will be rusty but drinkable after it has been properly purified.

open the lowest furnace drain cock. To speed water flow, open or remove one or two air-bleed valves from top-floor radiators. The 25 or more gallons of water present in your heating system will be a little rusty and may have an odor. It can be used as is for washing but must be purified before you can drink it. Purification is discussed shortly.

If your home has a steam-heat system, you can drain the water contained there. There won't be much, but it's all water.

Still another possible source of water within your home is a sump pump. Remove the cover to the sump and bail out whatever water may be there. Frequently, more water will collect as you do this. If you still have electric power and wish to go to the trouble of dismantling a portion of the sump pump's drainpipe, you can arrange for the pump to supply you with water. However, if the sump's drain is connected to the house drainpipe, it is inadvisable to do this. Some of the pathogenic bacteria will have worked their way back into the drainpipe, in which case the water must be purified before consumption.

Outdoor sources of water. Rain water is pure. You can drink whatever you can collect. Set out pots and pans when it rains and try bending the leaders coming down from the gutters so that you can collect whatever rain falls on the roof.

Dew is also drinkable, but if animals have been active on your lawn, you will have to purify the dew first. Take a baking tin or similar pan and skim the dew from the top of the grass. Dew forms just when the cold night air hits the earth.

Water from local wells that have been flooded can still be used, but the water must first be purified.

Water can sometimes be secured from shallow wells that are no longer operative because of power failure by removing the well covers and dropping a small

A sump can be a source of drinking water. Be certain to purify the water before using if the sump pump connects directly to the sewer line, or if there is a septic tank within 50 feet or so of the sump.

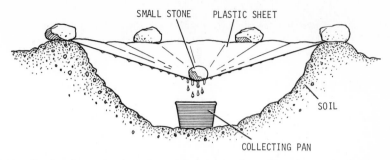

SMALL STONE   PLASTIC SHEET

SOIL

COLLECTING PAN

System for drawing water from the earth. It is slow but will work even in the desert.

pail on a hand line. Sometimes you can arrange to turn the associated pump by hand. *Be certain to turn the power off first;* otherwise, an unexpected return of electric power can take your hand with it. Also, open the associated air valve so that you are just pumping water up from the well and not developing pressure to drive the water through the house.

Water from nearby streams can, of course, also be used. But in these days of massive stream pollution, wait until all your other water is gone, unless you have a clear stream.

There is a good chance you will uncover ground water within a few feet if you dig in a low-lying, damp area near lush, natural growth. Your well need not be anything more than a hole. Slope its sides so that they do not fall in, and continue digging for a foot or so after you strike water. Then let the water clear itself by standing and bail off the top layer of water carefully. If you are more than 50 feet from a cesspool or septic tank, you can drink the water without purification.

Near salt water, dig your well 20 or so feet from the water's edge. As the sea water moves sideways through the sand to your well, most of the salt will be left behind. You can drink brackish water, but never drink sea water. It can kill you. If you have the time and the strength, dig a second well farther inland. The water you uncover there will be sweeter.

In dry areas, if there is little or no vegetation, and you are not close to a sea, your chances of digging down to water are somewhat less than slim. However, there is a way of extracting water from desert soil. Dig a hole several feet deep and several feet across. Place a pan in the bottom of the hole. Spread a sheet of plastic across the hole and hold the edges of the sheet in place with stones. Place another stone in the center of the sheet above the pan. This will make the sheet sag downward a bit. When the sun strikes the plastic it will warm the space beneath it. Moisture will be drawn from the earth, condense on the underside of the sheet and drip into the pan. Not a fountain, but drinking water nonetheless. This water can be drunk without further treatment.

Clarification. Cloudy or slightly muddy water is not necessarily dangerous to drink. At the same time, sparkling clear water is not necessarily pure and safe to drink. To clarify cloudy or muddy water let the water stand overnight and pour off the top, clear layer. You can also pour the water repeatedly through clean

Water can be cleared, but not puri-fied, by pouring it through a cloth.

cloths or make a filter from clean sand and pour the water through it. The last can be accomplished by placing clean sand in a funnel atop a piece of cloth.

Odor can be removed from water by adding a little charcoal or ashes from a wood fire to the water and then boiling it.

Purification. Boil the water for 3 minutes or more. If you are using the water for cooking and this will include 3 minutes of boiling, no further treatment is necessary. Another possibility is to add Halazone, iodine, or chlorine tablets to the water following the instructions. These tablets are sold in camping supply shops. You can also add 2 drops of any laundry bleach consisting of a 5- to 6-percent solution of sodium hypochlorite and water to every quart of clear water you wish to purify or 4 drops to every quart of cloudy water you wish to purify. (Purex, Clorox, Rose-X, and other commercial bleaches contain the proper chemicals.) Let the bleach and water mixture stand for 30 minutes. If you can detect a slight chlorine odor, it is ready to drink. If not, repeat the dosage and let the water stand for another 15 minutes. Note that water which you have not so treated but which has a chlorine odor is safe to drink.

As an alternative you can add 5 drops of 2-percent tincture of iodine to each quart of clear water or.10 drops to each quart of cloudy water and let it stand for 30 minutes. You will generally find iodine in this strength in your medicine cabinet or first aid kit. If the percentage of iodine is higher or lower than 2 percent, vary the dosage accordingly.

WINDOWS

Cracked pane. As long as the pane of glass does not come apart it is possible to make an emergency repair that will hold the pieces in place until you are able to properly replace the pane. This is the way it may be done.

Gently wipe the pane of glass clean along both sides of the crack on both sides of the pane. Place the open end of a tube of Duco cement against the crack and move the tube along the crack, squeezing out and laying down a narrow film of cement. Repeat this operation on the other side of the crack. When the cement on one side of the pane passes through the crack and bonds to the cement on the other side, a plastic clamp results that holds the pieces fairly securely in place.

Broken pane. To patch a hole in a windowpane, clean the surface of the glass around the hole for a width of a few inches. Then spread Duco cement over the cleaned area and lightly press a piece of glass, larger than the hole, against the cement. Hold the piece of glass in place until you are certain the cement has hardened. In cold weather, warm the piece of glass before you position it to speed the setting of the cement.

Stuck window, double-hung. Work a flat knife between the window frame and the sash for the entire circumference of the sash (the frame in which the glass is supported). If that doesn't loosen the sash, make a cleat from a piece of wood about 2 inches wide and 8 inches long. Fasten this to the lower portion of the sash in a horizontal position with two wood screws. Place a second small board, about the size of the cleat, on the window sill. Place the end of a long board against the window sash and beneath the cleat. Lower the other end of the board and force the cleat and window sash to move upwards.

A faster but more damaging alternative is to drive the tip of a strong screwdriver into the bottom of the sash, just above the window sill. A small piece of wood is placed on the sill beneath the screwdriver shaft. Then the handle of the driver is forced downward, the lever action hopefully raising the window. You may have to repeat this action at several points across the bottom of the sash.

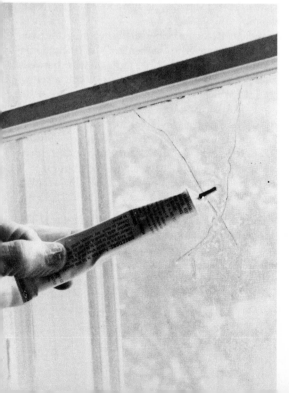

The trick to making cracked glass remain in place with cement alone is to apply the cement to both sides of the cracks.

When you cannot budge a window by any other means, fasten a cleat to it and use a lever to raise it.

If you don't have a screwdriver handy, but do have an ax, drive the point of the ax into the sash near the sill, then use the ax as a lever with or without a small piece of wood underneath.

Stuck slider. Sliding windows stick when they jump their track, run over an obstruction in the track or cock in their frames.

In the first case, you can sometimes force the window back into its track by prying it upwards gently with a screwdriver. Moving the window back and forth a little as you do this sometimes helps.

Obstructions under a window can sometimes be removed by working the window back and forth until the obstruction is moved to one end of the track. Sometimes the obstruction can be removed by running a stiff length of wire between the track and the window while you pry the window upwards a bit with a screwdriver. Sometimes the only way consists of bending a little hook on the end of the wire and fishing the obstruction out. In all cases you have to be careful not to place pressure on the glass. Sliding windows are easily cracked.

Windows cock and refuse to move because there is too much space between the window and its frame. With a screwdriver gently return the window to its horizontal position. Then, if possible, line the bottom or upper track with a thin strip of plastic (nylon preferably) to reduce the clearance and hold the window in place.

Storm windows. Storm windows are useless if there is a hole in the glass. The purpose of the window is to provide a pocket of nonmoving air. Moving air carries heat with it. Nonmoving air insulates. Therefore you must seal the opening in the window one way or another. See Broken pane.

If the glass is completely gone or if you have no storm window and need one in a hurry, cover the entire window frame (this is done inside the building) with a clear sheet of plastic. Use tacks or masking tape to seal the plastic to the window frame.

114

Index